This is
MOZAMBIQUE

This is
MOZAMBIQUE

Ian Michler

First published in 1999 by New Holland Publishers (UK) Ltd
London * Cape Town * Sydney * Auckland
2 4 6 8 10 9 7 5 3 1

24 Nutford Place
London W1H 6DQ
United Kingdom

80 McKenzie Street
Cape Town 8001
South Africa

14 Aquatic Drive
Frenchs Forest
NSW 2086, Australia

218 Lake Road
Northcote, Auckland
New Zealand

Managing editor: Annlerie van Rooyen
Editor: Glynne Newlands
Design manager: Janice Evans
Designer & cover design: Sonia Hedenskog de Villiers
Cartographer: Anton Krugel
Proofreader and indexer: Claudia Dos Santos
Consultant: Austral Consultant Group (Time Out).– Polly Gaster
Reproduction by Hirt & Carter Cape (Pty) Ltd
Printed and bound by Tien Wah Press (Pte) Limited, Singapore

Front cover: *A dhow leaves the shores of Vilanculos.*
Spine: *Wimbe beach, Pemba.*
Frontispiece: *A Makua girl from the Palma district.*
Title page: *The parish church of San Antonio on Ilha de Moçambique.*
This page: *Dhows at anchor at Maxixe in Inhambane Bay.*
Contents page: *The palm-lined beach of Wimbe, Pemba.*
Overleaf: *Seascape, Benguerra Island.*

CONTENTS

AUTHOR'S DEDICATION

The making of this book has been a most thrilling and rewarding experience. The fact that I came upon the opportunity by chance, rather than by dedicated planning, has made it all the more exciting. In April 1997 I had the good fortune of accompanying a great friend on a short trip to the coastal regions of Inhambane Province, joining him at the last minute. Part of our journey took us to the secluded 'ponta' of Linga Linga, and while strolling along its unspoiled beaches, the idea for this book was born. Thank you, Jez.

It was only after taking the decision to go ahead with this project and after having done the initial research that I realised the enormity of the task. Although I have attempted to cover as much of Mozambique as possible and offer a truly a representative portrayal of the country and its people, it is by no means a complete work, but rather a window into the country. Because of logistical and geographical difficulties in reaching certain far-flung regions and because of the tragic issue of landmines in the rural areas, there are parts of the country I was unable to cover. Also, trying to gather statistical data and updated information that is consistent in its detail has been problematic, primarily because these figures are often outdated or do not even exist, and because many departments do not have the structures in place to perform this task. I hope these shortcomings will not detract from the book, and my only regret is that I was not able to spend more time in the country's embrace.

So many people gave of their time and advice in helping me put this book together. Besides the government officials, private consultants, businessmen and women, tour operators, lodge and hotel staff and many others, I would like to express my gratitude to the people of Mozambique for their immense hospitality, generosity of character and fervent enthusiasm towards my cameras and myself. They are truly spirited folk and the heartening recovery Mozambique has made over the last decade is, without doubt, built on the positive and courageous attitude of its most valuable asset, the Mozambican people. I dedicate this book to them and the many who are so boldly involved in putting together the brittle pieces of the past, and hope that, in some small way, it will help to pass on the message to the rest of the world that Mozambique is back in the fold. Obrigado – Kanimambo.

ACKNOWLEDGEMENTS

I am especially grateful to the following organizations and people for their assistance: the Government of Mozambique and the Cabinet of Information, especially Manuel Zavala, for granting me permission to undertake the project; the Directorate of Tourism and its national director, Arlindo Langa, for their unqualified endorsement; Direccão Nacional de Florestas e Fauna Bravia (DNFFB) in Maputo and Beira for allowing me access to their magnificent wilderness areas; the governors of each of the provinces; the National History Archive for unearthing history books in English; the World Bank for providing statistics; and Ishaci Abdul Aly Baraca, the administrator on Ilha de Moçambique;

The foundation of the country's tourism industry lies in its hotels, lodges and tour operators. The following have been immensely generous in allowing me the use of their facilities:

The Polana Hotel, the Cardoso Hotel and the Rovuma Carlton in Maputo; Pestana Hotels and Resorts for flying me across to Inhaca Hotel and Bazaruto Lodge; Richard and Colette Fair of Nkomati Safaris and the Elephant Coast Co; Incomati River Camp at the mouth of the Incomati River; Zongoene Lodge on the Limpopo River mouth; Barra Lodge at Ponta da Barra; Marlin Lodge and Benguerra Lodge on Benguerra Island; Indigo Bay Lodge on Bazaruto Island; Vilankulo Beach Lodge in Vilanculos; the Hotel Embaixador in Beira; Casa Msika on the shores of Chicamba Real Dam; Ugezi Tiger Lodge upstream from Cahora Bassa Dam; Univendas Apartments in Tete; Hotel Chuabo in Quelimane; Hotel Tropical in Nampula; Complexo Turístico and Naútilus in Pemba; Restaurante and Bar São Miguel in Cuamba; Morrungulo Lodge; Casa Lisa a short distance north of Maputo, and Motel do Mar in Ponta do Ouro.

Numerous individuals gave invaluable advice and hospitality: Judy Greathead at the South African Embassy; Paul and Sheila Dutton; Jeremy Anderson; Chris and David Greathead; Ross Douglas; Koos and Retha Human; Julio Maela; Silverio Sitoe; Ricky Jacobs of Mozambique Island Tours; Dee-Jean Travel Promotions; Antonio Matos and Jeanne Stephens from Austral Publications; Gerhard Leisegang at the Eduardo Mondlane University; Nigel Pollard, Emanuel Lourenço and Carlos Silva from Grupo Madal; James Riley, curator of the Palace Museum on Ilha de Moçambique; Mark and Clare Jenkins from the Niassa Reserve; Roberto Zolho from Gorongosa National Park; John-Boy Mauvis and Peter Thornycroft of Organizacões Palmeiras Ltda; Father Marques Antonio Rafael; Joachim and Sieglinde Gessner from Quirimba Island Lodge; Janine Moallic from Ibo Island; Nick Bateman from the Halo Trust, and Matthew Khoury and Nadia and Kerenn.

Two Mozambican companies have been the backbone of this project and without their support it would not have been possible. Hernáni Mata and the Toyota De Moçambique team allowed me the use of a diesel Toyota Landcruiser 4x4 with which I covered over 12,000 kilometres (7,500 miles) without a single problem. Jos Scherrenberg and BP Oil Moçambique Limited kept my vehicle well oiled via their extensive network of service stations. I now know why they are the leaders in their respective sectors. To them: expressions of sincere gratitude and the biggest thank-you.

To Ken Patrick and Agfa South Africa: a big thank-you, too, for sponsoring the film (Agfachrome RSX 100 Professional) for this book, the results of which are visible in the great colour saturation and vivid tones of the photographs.

PROFILE OF MOZAMBIQUE

Opposite: *Fresh spinach being brought to the central market in Manica. Vegetables are grown by subsistence farmers in the valleys surrounding the town.*
Above: *Sunset over Mount Gorongosa. The range's highest peak is 1,863 metres (6,112 feet).*

Blessed with unspoiled beaches, magnificent coral reefs, superb seafood and a relaxed atmosphere, Mozambique's enduring attributes all contributed to the country's former reputation as an ideal holiday destination. This status was established during the 1960s and early 1970s when Southern Africa was still a region of white privilege, but in 1975 Mozambique gained independence, an event which had a profound effect on the country's growth and stability.

The new government adopted socialist policies and became a front-line area in the worldwide fight against white minority rule and apartheid. A period of external aggression and war ensued, lasting until the early 1990s, closing the chapter on what had become for many South African, Portuguese and formerly Rhodesian families a traditional pilgrimage to the country's celebrated coastline and its two major cities, Maputo and Beira.

It was during these two decades of protracted conflict that Mozambique became Africa's forgotten land, abandoned by the tourists and investors of the world.

Thankfully for the country and its people, that tragic period of war in its long, and at times traumatic, history is over. The nation has entered a period of rebuilding, embarking on a path of economic growth and development to ensure that Mozambique will, once again, become a prominent member of the African continent. Today, the only obvious signs of the past are the numerous decaying buildings in the cities and towns, as well as the many streets and buildings still bearing names of famous Marxist and liberation leaders.

The dawning of peace has heralded the chance for the world to rediscover the splendour of Mozambique. The country, which took its name from Ilha de Moçambique, a small island off the northern coast named after the Arab sultan Moussa Ben Mbiki, consists of so much more than just beautiful beaches and excellent cuisine.

The eastern end of the Zambezi Gorge lies approximately 2 kilometres (1¼ miles) from the Cahora Bassa Dam wall.

It offers an intriguing historical study, a rich cultural diversity, spectacular wilderness landscapes, one of the world's best underwater realms, and a people who are known for their great fortitude and warmth.

Possessing an exotic blend of Arabic, African and European influences, Mozambique has melded into a unique society with a distinctive style and identity, and is endowed with an ambience not experienced elsewhere in Southern and East Africa.

For those who know the country and its numerous attractions, the enduring beauty and unsophisticated charm of Mozambique remains a constant lure. And for the first-time visitor, a wealth of exciting and absorbing discoveries await.

THE LAND

Located on the southeastern coast of Africa, between latitudes 10 and 26 degrees south and longitudes 30 and 41 degrees east, Mozambique is bordered to the south by South Africa and Swaziland, to the west by Zimbabwe, Zambia and Malawi, and to the north by Tanzania. It is separated from Madagascar, 300 kilometres (190 miles) to the east, by the Mozambique Channel. Mozambique covers an area of approximately 799,380 square kilometres (308,653 square miles), which includes 13,000 square kilometres (5,020 square miles) of inland water, the major part comprising the Cahora Bassa Dam and the country's portion of Lake Niassa, shared with Malawi and Tanzania.

The outstanding geographical feature of Mozambique is its long, pristine coastline of 2,515 kilometres (1,563 miles), washed by the warm waters of the Indian Ocean. Extending the full length of the coast are numerous smallish islands, many of which were, at some stage, a part of the mainland. The best known of these island groups, because of their popularity as holiday destinations, are Inhaca Island, the Bazaruto Archipelago and the Quirimbas Archipelago; and Ilha de Moçambique, because of its important cultural and historical background. The coastline and its islands are almost exclusively comprised of coral rock, sandy beaches, sheltered bays, some protected by outlying coral reefs, and sand spits. As the sand spits allow easy access from the mainland to the islands, over 60 per cent

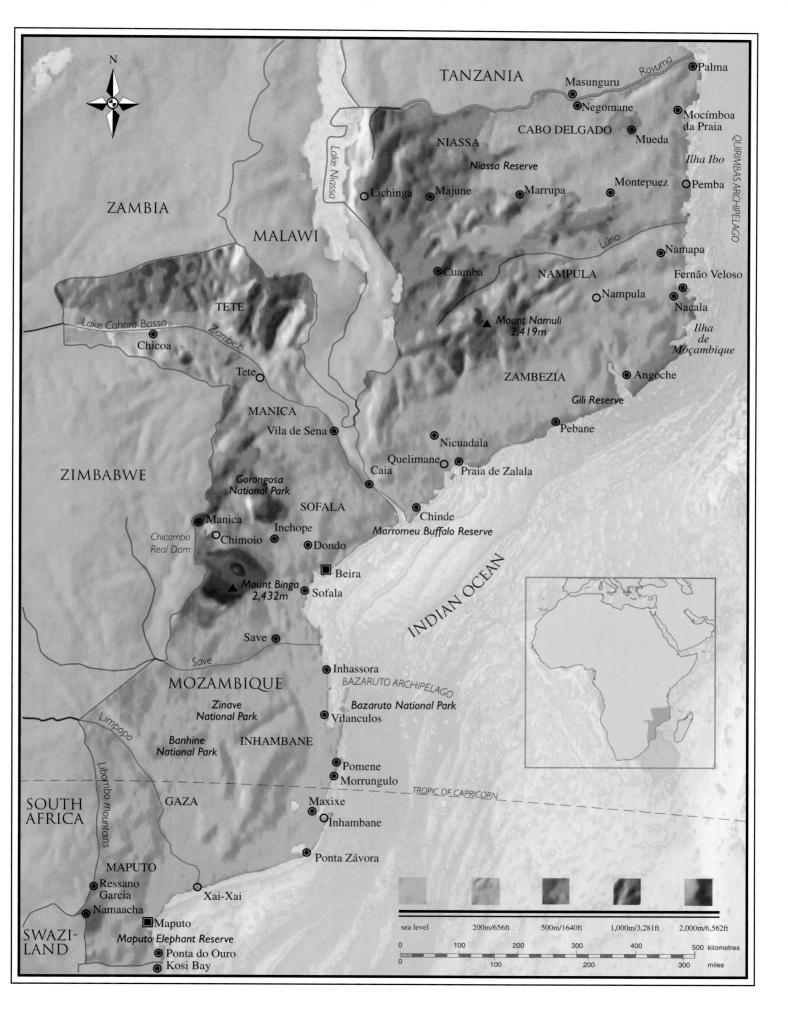

N

TANZANIA

Rovuma

Palma

Masunguru

Negomane

CABO DELGADO

Mocímboa
da Praia

Mueda

QUIRIMBAS ARCHIPELAGO

NIASSA

Niassa Reserve

Ilha Ibo

Lake Niassa

Lichinga   Majune   Marrupa   Montepuez   Pemba

Namapa

ZAMBIA

Cuamba

NAMPULA

Fernão Veloso

MALAWI

Nampula

Nacala

TETE

Mount Namuli
2,419m

Ilha
de
Moçambique

Lake Cahora Bassa   Zambezi

Chicoa

ZAMBEZIA

Angoche

Tete

Gili Reserve

MANICA

Vila de Sena

Pebane

ZIMBABWE

Nicuadala

Gorongosa
National Park

Quelimane   Praia de Zalala

Caia

SOFALA

Manica

Chinde

Chimoio   Inchope

Marromeu Buffalo Reserve

Chicamba
Real Dam

Dondo

Beira

Mount Binga
2,432m

Sofala

INDIAN OCEAN

Save

MOZAMBIQUE

Inhassora

BAZARUTO ARCHIPELAGO

Zinave
National Park

Bazaruto National Park

Banhine
National Park

INHAMBANE

Vilanculos

Limpopo

Pomene

Morrungulo

TROPIC OF CAPRICORN

SOUTH
AFRICA

Libombo mountains

GAZA

Maxixe

Inhambane

Ponta Závora

MAPUTO

Ressano
Garcia

Xai-Xai

Namaacha

Maputo

SWAZI-
LAND

Maputo Elephant Reserve

Ponta do Ouro

Kosi Bay

sea level   200m/656ft   500m/1640ft   1,000m/3,281ft   2,000m/6,562ft

0   100   200   300   400   500 kilometres

0   100   200   300 miles

of the country's population lives along the coast, many making a living from its marine resources.

Geologists believe that about 125,000 years ago the country's southern and central lowlands lay beneath the sea, and that various Ice Ages (the most recent being 7,000 years ago), caused the sea level to recede to its present position. This belief is strongly supported by fossil finds and the various geographical features occurring today. Not only have fossilized crustaceans been found along the edges of the Libombo Mountain range, roughly 120 kilometres (75 miles) inland from the present sea level, but many of the numerous inland lakes and their surrounding sand habitats have fairly high salinity levels, remnants of the receding primeval ocean, whose waters became trapped in the lower lying areas.

Topographically the country consists of four main sections – essentially a series of belts which decrease in altitude from the interior to the Indian Ocean. In the northern and extreme western regions, and comprising about 12 per cent of the country, is a mountainous zone consisting of sandstone, granite and gneiss rock which exceeds altitudes of 1,000 metres (3,280 feet), with several peaks above 2,000 metres (6,562 feet). The Makonde Plateau in the north, the Tete Highlands in the northwest and the Gorongosa Highlands, Penhalonga and Vumba ranges in the west are the prominent mountains, making up most of the montane areas. Mozambique's highest peak, Mount Binga (2,436 metres [7,992 feet]), lies in the isolated Chimanimani range and few people have ventured up its slopes.

Adjoining the highlands and covering roughly 26 per cent of the country, the landscape descends towards what is known as the high plateau region (areas of between1,000 and 600 metres

In Maputo, taxis are the most popular form of transport for getting to work.

[3,280 and1,970 feet] in altitude) which includes the Northeastern Escarpment. Moving further eastwards is the medium plateau belt, an area of gently undulating granite hills ranging in altitudes of between 600 and 200 metres (1,970 and 660 feet) and which comprises about 18 per cent of the land. The remaining 44 per cent of the country is lowland, consisting of savanna plains, marshland, dune forests and the coastline. It includes two major sedimentary basins, the Rovuma Basin in the north and the larger Mozambique Basin extending to the very south, both caused by tectonic movement in the earth's crust. The southern extent of the Great East African Rift Valley, the vast fault line that runs the length of the eastern side of Africa, cuts through the central parts of Mozambique.

The northern regions of the country are covered predominantly by brachystegia and acacia woodland, subtropical

and riverine forest and savanna grassland, while dry forest, acacia woodland, savanna grassland and coastal dune forest dominate the provinces south of the Beira/Zimbabwe axis. Mangrove swamp is a feature of most of the coastline north of Maputo, particularly around river mouths and along estuarine channels.

One of the ironies of Mozambique's geography is that although there seems to be ample water if you consider Cahora Bassa Dam, Lake Niassa and the ten major rivers – all with numerous smaller inter-linked drainage patterns – the country still regularly suffers extreme droughts. The most impressive of the rivers, the mighty Zambezi, rises in the Angolan Highlands on the western side of the continent before entering Mozambique along its border with Zambia and Zimbabwe. It flows across 820 kilometres (510 miles) of countryside before forming a lush and swampy delta at its mouth, north of Beira.

The Maputo, Save, Buzi, Incomáti, Limpopo, Revue, Púngoè, Lúrio and the Rovuma are the other important rivers, with their sources in the higher central regions of the continent. They traverse vast regions of the Kalahari Basin and carry its sands in their flow eastwards, depositing them as sediments on reaching the lower lying plains of Mozambique. Thus the dominant upper soil covering the lowland regions is predominantly of the Kalahari sand type, a result of the many major river systems that have their mouths along this section of the country's coastline.

THE PEOPLE

An attempt to categorize the people of Mozambique is a complex and inexact exercise as, throughout its history, the country has been shaped by foreign influences, resulting in a unique culture of its own. Although not a homogenous society, one of the country's greatest strengths is the fact that the majority of its citizens are not overly concerned with cultural and ethnic divisions, but rather view themselves as Mozambicans entitled to practise their own customs.

The various influences go back to the movements of the powerful Bantu-speaking people in the first century A.D. before the Arab and Indian empires brought their identities to bear on Mozambique from around the 8th and 9th centuries. Probably the most influential interactions occurred over the long period of colonization (1498 to 1975) by the Portuguese.

While their political hold on the country was unforgiving, the Portuguese left a legacy that has mingled their language and lifestyle with that of the African people, an enriching blend that sits comfortably today, particularly with the more educated section of Mozambican society. Interracial relationships, and sometimes marriage, were more common than in many British colonies, and were, perhaps, the most harmonious element in the liaison between

colonizer and colonized. To a lesser degree has been the influence of the Chinese, Germans and English in the last century.

In recent times the country's experiment with Marxism brought it in touch with the ideas and systems of the communist world. Even the war has had a lasting effect on the country's culture, as it disrupted and destroyed many of the rural communities, and refugees returning from exile brought with them inheritances from their interim homes. As a result, traditional definitions have become blurred and, in some cases, lost with the combined effects of historical conquests and the movements of the Mozambican people. Today, many of the existing divisions are based on linguistic variations, geographical conditions and the more contemporary definitions of political alliance and class structure.

Mozambique has a population of over 16 million people, predominantly made up of ten different ethnic groups, some of which have cultural subdivisions. The Makua people from the northern provinces are the largest group, forming approximately 40 per

cent of the population, with the Tsonga in the south the second biggest, comprising roughly 25 per cent of the population. The Chope, Shona, Sena, Nyanja and Nyungue of the central provinces are all smaller groups, together making up 25 per cent of the population. The Chuabo, Yao, Ndau and Makonde make up the remainder.

The Ronga around Maputo, the Shangaan throughout the south, and the Tsua from Inhambane are all subdivisions of the Tsonga group. The Manyika are a small splinter group occurring in the Beira district, as are the Tawara around Cahora Bassa and the Ngoni in the far northwestern corners of Niassa. The Nampula, Zambezia and Maputo provinces carry the highest population densities, while those of Niassa and Tete have the lowest. A small percentage of the population consists of various minority groups of which the Portuguese are the largest, the others being Indian and Chinese who mostly live in the more developed urban centres of Maputo, Beira, Quelimane and Nampula.

Mozambicans are proud of their roots. The Makonde, who inhabit the far northern regions of the country, still dance in colourful costumes and masks, and carve as they always have, although the traditional art of tattooing the face and body is dying out. The Makua women of the northern coastal regions continue to paint their faces with a paste made from root extract, which together with the multi-coloured *capulanas* they wear, fashions an appealing aesthetic. Even today, Chope menfolk from Inhambane Province and Sena men from Sofala and Manica provinces, look for any reason to assemble a group of *marimba* players, often involving the whole village in an evening of song and dance.

Rural customs, such as pottery, weaving and brewing, and traditions such as ritual marriages and initiations, are still widespread throughout the country. Traditional healers, or *curandeiros*, remain influential and highly respected members of the community, a role

Party time at a local bar in Muturara. The Mozambican people have a wonderful sense of revelry with weekends being a time for song and dance.

that increased during the war years when many of the local leaders were foreced to flee to safety.

Portuguese is the official language of the country, although it is not generally spoken in the countryside, and there are thirteen main local languages with many dialects. The spread of Swahili, the widely spoken East African language, has been substantial in the north along the Rovuma River and the coastal regions as far south as Ilha de Moçambique.

Religious beliefs still remain predominantly traditional, although about 20 per cent of the population, mainly those from the urban areas, is Catholic, and another 25 per cent are Muslim, mainly along the coastal regions north of Beira.

In the urban centres and cities, world-renowned artists such as Malangatana and Silverio Sitoe depict with honesty and irony the cultural crossovers that have shaped the country's ways. Writers such as Mia Couto and José Craveirinha speculate on what might have been and what is to come for the next generation, and along with the many talented musicians and film-makers, are forging a new culture for the Mozambique of tomorrow.

The author's sponsored Toyota is ferried across the Shire River in northern Mozambique.

GETTING AROUND

For a country of this size, Mozambique has a disproportionately low number of good, surfaced roads and functional railway lines. At the time of writing, only 21 per cent of its 29,000 kilometres (18,020 miles) of main and secondary roads were paved, and less than a quarter of the country was serviced by rail. Moving around the country is demanding and requires good planning and patience. The southern half of the

country is better served, with the north-south coastal road (the EN1) connecting Maputo and Beira, and two main roads linking the country to South Africa and Zimbabwe, all in good condition. Any road journey through the central and northern regions is a slow, arduous experience as these provinces have poorly developed transport networks, with those roads that are surfaced in a state of disrepair.

Crossing the Zambezi River in the summer months can become a frustrating event as the bridge at Tete is the only reliable one, although there are three potential crossing points. A combination of heavy rains, mud-churned roads and dysfunctional barges seem to conspire annually to making the crossings at Vila de Sena and Caia nothing short of a time-consuming nightmare. Those who do not have the time or stomach for taking on the adventurous route north across the Zambezi River can make use of the well-maintained road that goes via Tete and Malawi, re-entering Mozambique at Milange in Zambezia Province.

The railway network consists primarily of three major lines running from the three major ports – Maputo, Beira and Nacala – linking them to South Africa, Zimbabwe and Malawi respectively. A few secondary lines, most of which operate on a sporadic basis, connect outlying towns to these centres. The state airline, Linhas Aéreas de Moçambique (LAM) is supported by various private charter companies who make use of over 200 airports, of which Maputo, Beira, Pemba and Vilanculos have international status.

THE CLIMATE

Lying predominantly within the tropics, with only Maputo Province and the southern regions of Gaza and Inhambane located south of the Tropic of Capricorn, Mozambique has a dual climate – tropical in the north and subtropical in

One of the country's busiest rail routes runs between Nampula and Mozambique's neighbour, Malawi. These passengers boarded the train at Cuamba.

The Limpopo floodplains are a major banana growing area. Bananas, an important subsistence crop, are sold in most cities and towns.

the south. Although Mozambique has no consistent climatic pattern, there are two distinguishable main seasons: the hot, rainy season, extending from October to March, and the cooler, dry season from April to September. Visitors to the country, particularly those wishing to enjoy the pleasures of its coastline, will find the cooler winter months a more comfortable period to travel, not only because of the more amenable weather conditions, but also because the threat of malaria during this period is greatly reduced.

The average monthly summer temperatures for the country vary between 27–31 °C (80–88 °F), and the winter averages between 18–21 °C (65–70 °F). Temperatures vary on a regional basis, with the north generally experiencing hotter and more humid summer conditions, daytime temperatures consistently reaching the mid-40 °Cs (about 115 °F) along the Zambezi Valley. But not

everywhere in Mozambique is subjected to the searing summer heat. The coastline is usually cooled by onshore winds and, because of higher altitudes, the western side of the central regions and parts of the far north have more moderate temperatures.

Mozambique's weather patterns are influenced by various factors such as the Indian Ocean monsoons, tropical equatorial air flows, the warm Mozambican current and the increase in elevation to the west of the country, all of which affect the wind and rainfall. Rainfall statistics show that the northern provinces receive a far higher mean annual average of 1,500 millimetres (60 inches), while the southern provinces receive 750 millimetres (30 inches), the divide being roughly along the Save River.

As summer rains in the south are irregular, this region is prone to drought and occasional floods that can cause considerable damage. During the

periods 1982–1984, 1986–1987 and 1992, the country, and especially the south, suffered severe droughts, resulting in famine and starvation. Although cyclone activity, particularly in the northern provinces, is not uncommon during the summer rainy season, the storms seldom reach levels capable of causing extensive damage.

THE PROVINCES

Mozambique is made up of eleven provinces, ten of which are divided into districts with each district functioning at local level through localities and administrative posts. These ten provinces are extensive regions, each with their own capital and administrative systems, while the eleventh is the city of Maputo (formerly Lourenço Marques), deemed to be a province of its own because of its population size and administrative needs.

The upmarket Cardoso Hotel affords an impressive view over Maputo Bay.

MAPUTO CITY

Situated in Maputo Province, the capital city is a cosmopolitan mix of all the groups found in Mozambique, and most of the country's Portuguese descendants and expatriates live and work here. Some 602 square kilometres (232 square miles) in size, Maputo is fast reclaiming its reputation as one of the continent's finest metropolitan areas. The city's impressive skyline of recently renovated architectural landmarks and skyscrapers looms over the waters of Maputo Bay. Built on two levels and serviced by an efficient network of broad, leafy avenues, the city's business and administration sectors meet at the downtown junction of Av. 25 de Setembro and Av. Samora Machel, while embassies, foreign development agencies and Maputo's citizens live uptown, overlooking the bay and harbour. The continual movement of tankers and cargo ships in and out of what has again become an important Southern African port can be seen from many vantage points.

MAPUTO PROVINCE

The smallest of the remaining ten provinces (25,756 square kilometres [9,945 square miles] in size), Maputo Province covers the area south of the Limpopo River, and is bordered by Gaza to the north, the Indian Ocean to the east, South Africa to the south and Swaziland and South Africa to the west. Matola is its capital, and the population of roughly one million is made up of the Shangaan and Ronga groups. Inland from the belt of coastal dune forest, the terrain is uniformly flat throughout and is characterized by savanna grassland and dry forest, with the southern plains holding numerous saline and freshwater lakes. The floodplains of the Incomati River provide fertile soils for the province's extensive sugar cane plantations. Other economic activity includes fishing, cattle and citrus farming, and tourism.

GAZA PROVINCE

The lifeblood of this province is the Limpopo River, flowing across the width of the region and entering the sea on the southern side of the area's capital city, Xai-Xai. Some 75,709 square kilometres (29,232 square miles) in size, Gaza Province has a population of about 1.5 million Shangaan and Chope people, and is bordered by Zimbabwe and Manica to the north, Inhambane to the east, the Indian Ocean and Maputo Province to the south, and South Africa to the west. Commercial and subsistence farmers cultivate the river's floodplains extensively to grow cashew nuts, rice and maize. The floodplains provide the only fertile soils in an otherwise dry province, the remainder of the area is covered with acacia and broad-leafed woodland.

INHAMBANE PROVINCE

This region of 68,615 square kilometres (26,493 square miles) is the tourist mecca of Mozambique as it includes the Bazaruto Archipelago and the popular section of coastline from Praia da Zavala to Inhassoro. Inhambane City is the capital of this province which has an estimated population of 1.25 million Chope and Tsonga people. It is bordered by Manica and Sofala to the north, the Indian Ocean to the south and east, and Gaza to the west. Stretching the length of the province's coast is a narrow band of dune forest and numerous inland saline and freshwater lakes, many of which are visible from the main coastal road heading north. Vast plantations of coconuts, bananas, cashew nuts and mango trees hug the roadside, giving Inhambane a lush, tropical feel. The western side of the province, extending up to the border on the Save River, is a mixture of dry forest and acacia woodland with several prominent stands of baobabs. Tourism plays a major role in the economy, and the main agricultural activities include cashew nut, coconut and citrus farming, and fishing.

SOFALA PROVINCE

Situated between the Zambezi River in the north and the Save River in the south, this central province has as its capital Mozambique's second largest city, Beira (estimated population 400,000). It is bordered by Tete, Malawi and Zambezia to the north, the Indian Ocean to the east, Inhambane to the south and Manica to the west, and is roughly 68,018 square kilometres (26,263 square miles) in size. Sofala's population of some 1.6 million is made up of the Sena and Ndau groups. Besides the two major rivers on the boundaries, this region has numerous smaller rivers, the Pŭngoè and Buzi being the largest, coursing their way across the low-lying plains and creating extensive swamp and marshland. The inland regions are covered by deciduous and semi-deciduous woodland and acacia forest, and the timber industry is thus one of the province's principal economic activities, others being fishing and sugar farming. Income is also earned from its port facilities.

MANICA PROVINCE

Approximately 61,661 square kilometres (23,808 square miles) in size, Manica Province is bordered by Tete to the north, Sofala to the east, Inhambane and Gaza to the south, and Zimbabwe to the west. Manica's capital is Chimoio and its population of some 900,000 people is made up of the Shona and Sena groups. A landlocked, mountainous province comprising the Penhalonga, Mavonde and Catandica ranges in the northwest and the Vumba and Tsetserra ranges in the southwest, the country's highest peak, Mount Binga (2,436 metres; 7,992 feet), is found in its southern ranges. The higher average altitude gives the province a more temperate

climate, suitable for growing tobacco and citrus fruit. Miombo woodland and riverine forest cover the lower-lying regions, and the timber industry is one of the main economic activities, as is gold mining.

TETE PROVINCE

Tete Province, about 100,724 square kilometres (38,891 square miles) in size, is bounded by Zambia to the north, Malawi to the east, Manica and Sofala to the south, and Zimbabwe to the west. Its capital is Tete City, and its population of approximately 1.1 million is comprised of the Nyungue and Nyanja people. This sparsely populated and landlocked province is home to the massive Cahora Bassa Dam and its hydroelectric power station built on the Zambezi River. Tete's vegetation ranges from deciduous and semi-decidious woodland in the south to acacia and mopane savanna and dry forest in the north. The province's income is mainly derived from hydroelectric power, coal, iron ore and the kapenta-fishing industry.

ZAMBEZIA PROVINCE

This is Mozambique's second largest province in terms of both population density (some 3,2 million) and size

(roughly 105,008 square kilometres; 40,545 square miles), and its capital is Quelimane. Zambezia is bordered by Niassa and Nampula to the north, the Indian Ocean to the east, Sofala to the south and Malawi to the west, and is populated by the Chuabo, Makua, Sena and Nyanja groups. The province has massive economic potential as the interior has rich deposits of semiprecious stones and minerals, such as tantalite. The coastal strip and its adjacent inland areas, fed by numerous river systems, have extremely fertile soils where coconuts, tea, timber and cotton are grown. Fishing forms another important part of the economy.

NAMPULA PROVINCE

Bordered by Cabo Delgado to the north, the Indian Ocean to the east, Zambezia to the south and Niassa to the northwest, Nampula Province, of which Nampula City is the capital, is inhabited by the Makua people. The province, the most densely populated in the country with an estimated 3,4 million people living in an area of around 81,606 square kilometres (31,509 square miles), offers a wealth of interesting and exciting options to the traveller. Besides the breathtaking scenery, the country's cultural melting pot, Ilha de Moçambique, lies within a short distance from the coastline. A visit to this island will confirm why the United Nations Educational, Scientific and Cultural Organization (UNESCO) and the Mozambique government proclaimed it a World Heritage Site in 1992: the countryside is a wonderland of towering granite inselberg formations spread among plains of miombo woodland and a patchwork of cotton and cashew nut plantations. Tobacco is another of the province's important crops.

NIASSA PROVINCE

This is the province of extremes, topping the list in various statistical categories. It is the largest province (129,056 square kilometres; 49,830 square miles), has the highest average altitude (about

Pods of baobab trees are for sale along the roadside in Tete Province.

700 metres [2,296 feet] above sea level), the lowest and most sparsely distributed population (780,000 people) and the least developed infrastructure. Tanzania forms Niassa's northern boundary, Cabo Delgado the eastern, Nampula and Zambezia the southern, and Malawi the western border. The capital of Niassa Province is Lichinga, and the Yao, Makua and Nyanja groups make up its population. Being so remote has had its advantages for the province: today, the vast wilderness area of the Niassa Reserve holds the largest remaining proportion of a wildlife population that was ravaged during the war years. The western highland region, known as the Lichinga Plateau, borders onto Lake Niassa. Cotton, maize, timber, semiprecious stones and fishing form the backbone of the province's economy.

CABO DELGADO PROVINCE

The country's most northerly province, bordered by Tanzania to the north, the Indian Ocean to the east, Nampula to the south and Niassa to the west, will forever be the pride of all Mozambicans. It was here that the fight for independence was launched with the fearless Makonde people at the forefront. Today, these warriors of the north are probably better known for their intricate carvings, sold in almost every curio market throughout the country. The other main group living here is the Makua people. Pemba is the capital of Cabo Delgado, and its population of about 1,3 million is involved in the timber, cotton, marble and fishing industries. The province, roughly 2,625 square kilometres (1,014 square miles) in extent, has some of the country's most appealing and unexplored coastline, which includes the string of tropical islands known as the Quirimba Archipelago. Moving inland from the narrow strip of coastal forest and mangrove swamp, the landscape rises gently towards the Mueda plateau in the west, covered predominantly by riverine forest and miombo woodland.

THE COUNTRY'S HIGHLIGHTS

MAPUTO AND SURROUNDS

The capital and hub of Mozambique is a large, sprawling city with a population of close on 2 million people. Maputo is an intriguing mosaic, fusing the worlds of old colonialism, first-world development, new African empowerment and third-world street life. Banks and corporate headquarters share their street addresses with local craft traders, while colonial homes nestle in the shadows of high-rise apartment buildings. European-style delicatessens trade opposite noisy open-air markets, and pushcarts switch traffic lanes with modern motor vehicles. The cogs of this unique city are kept moving by a population of all colours and creeds, who go about life at a relaxed pace that is within keeping of Africa's tradition.

Under colonial rule the city, known then as Lourenço Marques after a Portuguese trader and navigator of the same name, basked in a reputation of being one of Africa's finest. Fifteen years of strife, however, reduced it to a shadow of its former splendour. Today, Maputo is re-emerging as a vibrant metropolis of government, economic and cultural activity.

Although the aftermath of neglect is still clearly visible, much of the inner city has been, or is, in the process of being restored. Roads have been resurfaced, electricity and water supplies are now reliable, stately buildings have been refurbished, public and government facilities are open for business and certain residential neighbourhoods are again showing signs of affluence. Nowhere is Maputo's renewed vigour more prominent than in the city's nightclubs and restaurants. The citizens of Maputo have long been known for their sense of revelry and style, attributes that remain undiminished, and a night out on the town is an exciting blend of African flair and European charm.

The city is home to most aspects of Mozambican life. It is the seat of government and the judiciary, as well as the economy, and is the melting pot of a thriving cultural life. It is also the gateway for a majority of visitors. Numerous landmarks are spread around its limits, from the grand Catholic Cathedral and the interesting copper-domed railway station to the regal City Hall and the bustling Central Municipal Market. Maputo is well served by world-class hotels that welcome ever-increasing numbers of tourists and business people. The well-known Polana and Cardoso hotels, both lwith splendid views over the bay, have been joined by a third luxury hotel, the Rovuma Carlton, whose African style décor has added an in-vogue and relaxed option to the more gracious and traditional atmospheres of the other two.

A revival of Maputo's manufacturing and service industries is taking place in the city's immediate vicinity. The harbour, a pivotal element in the country's future economic growth, the international airport, oil refineries and countless factories are being upgraded and geared for better times. It is this infrastructure, along with the South African route from Nelspruit to Gauteng, that will play a crucial role in the development of what is known in economic terms as the Maputo Corridor. The country is basing much of its future aspirations on this development project, with its bilateral partner, the South African government. Maputo is within close proximity to two of Mozambique's major border posts: some 130 kilometres (80 miles) to the west, Ressano Garcia borderis on South Africa and is the country's busiest point of entry, while Namaacha, 80 kilometres (50 miles) from Maputo, lies on the border with Swaziland. Both are important links, as much of Mozambique's trade with South Africa is conveyed through them.

From Maputo, a three-hour ferry ride, one-hour speedboat trip or ten minutes by light aircraft travelling due east across the sea will bring you to Inhaca Island and its smaller neighbour, Portuguese Island. Inhaca forms the eastern rim of Maputo Bay, separated from the mainland by a 300-metre-wide (985 foot) channel of churning sea currents. From the manicured lawns encircling the swimming pool of the Inhaca Hotel, the island's only hotel and host to a constant flow of day-trippers and weekend visitors from Maputo, there is an impressive vista of the capital's shimmering skyline. A mere 500 metres (1,640 feet) north lies the tiny sanctuary of Portuguese Island, its uninhabited sandy shores offering respite for those wanting to escape Maputo's bustle.

The main attraction south of Maputo is the Maputo Elephant Reserve, once comprising 70,000 hectares (173,010 acres) but in 1996 incorporated into a large concession totalling 236,000 hectares

(583,292 acres). It now spreads from the southern tip of Inhaca Island to the country's southern border with South Africa. The terrain is distinctive in that it covers a wide spectrum of habitats, from rolling grass plains scattered with patches of sand and coastal dune forest to lagoons, swampy marshland and a lengthy stretch of untouched coastline. This territory was once ranged by large herds of elephant and plains game, as well as numerous predator species, but the reserve experienced steep declines in its animal populations due to extensive poaching and the effects of the war years. Crocodile, hippo and a variety of smaller creatures, such as side-striped jackal and duiker, were the only species that survived the slaughter.

In 1971, surveys accounted for over 350 elephant, the number falling to about 100 in the early 1990s before

herd numbers stabilized and began showing signs of recovery. Presently, the count is somewhere between 180 and 200. It was only through the vision of the Endangered Wildlife Trust, involved in the invaluable task of rehabilitating the reserve and its remaining wildlife, as well as working with local communities living on its fringes, that the elephant here were saved from total extermination. The enlarged concession area is now in the hands of the Elephant Coast Co., a joint venture company comprising the government, a private consortium and local communities, who are presently implementing a management plan to secure the wildlife populations and develop a sound ecotourism infrastructure.

Beyond the elephant reserve, some 120 kilometres (75 miles) south of Maputo, are the border towns of Ponta do Ouro and its neighbour, Ponta

This young boy learns the art of poling a dhow on the tranquil waters of Maxixe.

Guests at Barra Lodge can enjoy sunset cruises and day charters out at sea.

Malongane. These small coastal resorts, with their expansive beaches and inshore reefs, have become popular with South African scuba divers and fishermen. The most favoured resort is Ponta do Ouro, a throng of divers usually descending on the Motel do Mar and its dive school on the weekends.

The people of Maputo enjoy getting away from the city and a favourite destination is the Incomáti River Camp, tucked away on the banks of an isolated stretch of the Incomati River, about 30 kilometres (20 miles) north of the capital. The river meanders across a broad floodplain, a patchwork of natural marshland and subsistence crops, and through a series of oxbow bends before entering the sea on the outer limits of Maputo. Reaching the camp requires crossing the river by a manually hauled ferry that operates between the towns of Marracuene on the western bank and Macaneta on the eastern bank.

Forty-eight kilometres (30 miles) north of Maputo and conveniently positioned along the main road is the comfortable and homely lodge, Casa Lisa, a welcome overnight stop for visitors heading for the coastal resorts.

THE COAST
Xai-Xai

Situated on the northern bank of the Limpopo River, some 224 kilometres (140 miles) north of Maputo and 10 kilometres (6 miles) from the coastline, lies Xai-Xai. The main coastal road runs through the centre of town, a vibrant, bustling place and the first major stopover for travellers heading north. With its many well-stocked stores, filling stations and markets, the town allows those who wish to by-pass Maputo an opportunity to stock up on supplies.

A short hop over the undulating hills between town and coastline lies the better known side of Xai-Xai, the extensive beaches and turbulent seas of its coastal resort, the long-time favourite of both visitors and Maputo residents.

Not far from the town, on the southern bank at the mouth of the Limpopo, is the luxurious Zongoene Lodge. Tucked away from the prevailing winds, the lodge offers activities in scenic, tranquil surroundings. A boat cruise upriver from the lodge is a must, and affords a glimpse of local fishing communities at work among the imposing stands of mangrove trees lining both banks of the river.

Inhambane and Maxixe

Further north and set among extensive coconut palm groves is the city of Inhambane, the capital and administrative centre for Inhambane Province, and the town of Maxixe, the commercial centre for the region. Lying on opposite sides of Inhambane Bay, the two centres are linked by the constant flow of dhows and motorized taxi boats trafficking across 3,5 kilometres (2 miles) of sheltered waters. For road travellers, the trip is one of 60 kilometres (37,5 miles) as the road runs parallel to the long sweep of the bay. Although seemingly wide, the mouth of the bay is closed in by extensive sandbars stretching from both shores, leaving only a narrow channel of navigable water through which boats can enter.

On their first voyage around Africa, Vasco da Gama and his crew entered these waters and on landing at Inhambane, referred to the place as *terra de boa gente*, the land of the good people, in reference to the nature of the local Chope tribesman. This truism has endured the centuries and is now the maxim used by the local tourist association on their promotional material.

The city of Inhambane, the oldest city in the south, was established by the Portuguese as a trading post in 1534, and was also the southernmost reach of Arab traders before the arrival of the Portuguese. The now quiet and run-down streets with their many historical buildings radiate an aura of old-world charm and calmness. This is possibly the reason why, in more recent times, a number of writers and artists have made Inhambane their home.

Within a 20-kilometre (12,5-mile) radius of Inhambane are the beach resorts of Praia do Tofo, Praia dos Cocos and Ponta da Barra, each with their resident fishing communities and array of lodges and camp sites offering facilities for a variety of water sports. Especially enticing is the magnificent, unspoiled beach that stretches from the lighthouse at Ponta da Barra, past the front of Barra

Lodge, curving round into Inhambane Bay and ending in a string of narrow sand spits that choke the bay's mouth. Charter yacht cruises from Barra Lodge provide a wonderful chance to mill among the many grand dhows of the region as they gather at the mouth of the bay, fishing in a loose fleet-like formation.

Maxixe, a small town perched atop a gentle rise in the landscape, affords the clearest views across Inhambane Bay. The enduring vista is one of the bay's blue waters brimming with dhows, their patched white sails creating a perpetual wave of movement. These are the dhows of the many fishermen and sailors that work the bay's waters for a living.

Seventy-five kilometres (45 miles) north of Maxixe is the turn off to Morrungulo and the Complexo Turístico Morrungulo, an expansive resort nestled below a prime section of coastal dunes amid a healthy grove of coconut trees. It is very popular with South African and Zimbabwean deep-sea fishermen, offering ideal launching conditions and productive offshore fishing grounds for those in search of big game fish. To the north of Morrungulo the beach sweeps away in a lengthy arch, ending at Ponta da Barra Falsa, which also goes by the name of Pomene. At present, the Pestana Hotels and Resorts group have been entrusted with re-developing the once popular resort.

Vilanculos and Inhassoro

On an expansive stretch of coastline 700 kilometres (440 miles) north of Maputo lies the rapidly developing resort town of Vilanculos, set to become the heart of the burgeoning tourism industry in Mozambique. Not far offshore the Bazaruto Archipelago beckons. In the past Vilanculos served primarily as the gateway to the archipelago, but over the last few years the beachfront has attracted numerous new developments, making the town a destination in its own right. Vilanculos Beach Lodge is a fine example of the kind of development the government is encouraging in the country. Apart from being a sizeable investment and

Santa Carolina, or the 'Pearl of the Indian Ocean', is the smallest of the inhabited islands in the Bazaruto Archipelago.

aesthetically appealing, the lodge was built exclusively from local woods (primarily teak and ironwood), and has also played a major role in rejuvenating the local economy by manufacturing all furniture, basic fittings and structures on site, using Mozambican craftsmen.

Each rise and fall of the tide brings an ever-changing seascape to Vilanculos, alternately revealing calm, multi-hued seas or a myriad finely sculptured sandbars, giving the impression of an unbroken passageway between mainland and Archipelago. A walk onto the sandbars during spring low tide will reveal crustaceans and bring out feeding flocks of waders, while various species of game fish can be seen darting through the shallow channels. On the half tides, local fishermen return to the beaches to offload the day's catch, offering an assortment of fresh fish, lobster, squid and giant crabs for sale. For the adventurous, a dhow ride across the channel to one of the islands is a thrilling experience.

The small fishing village of Inhassoro is situated 94 kilometres (58 miles) north of Vilanculos. Not as scenically appealing as Vilanculos, the area is nevertheless

very popular with deep-sea fishermen who use the beaches to launch their ski boats and travel up to 40 kilometres (25 miles) out to the area's fishing grounds. The white sands from the islands of Santa Carolina and the northern tip of Bazaruto glisten a few kilometres offshore from Inhassoro.

The Bazaruto Archipelago

This group of five islands is the main attraction in Mozambique's array of enchanting beach destinations. The islands, strung out in a tapered chain along the coast from Vilanculos in the south to Inhassoro in the north, consist of Bazaruto in the north, 168 square kilometres (65 square miles) in size and by far the largest in the group, Benguerra in the middle, 33 square kilometres (12 square miles) in size and the second largest, and Magaruque in the south, stretching 9 square kilometres (3 square miles). Bangue, which is no more than an uninhabited sandy outcrop half a square kilometre (half a square mile) in size, lies on Magaruque's southern fringe. Santa Carolina, at 7 square kilometres (2,7 square miles) the smallest and oldest of the inhabited islands, is situated mid-distance between the mainland and the northern end of Bazaruto.

Other than Santa Carolina, which has a base of fossil rock dating back about 120,000 years, the islands are composed of dunes on the seaward side and lowlying sand flats and estuaries on the landward side. Numerous freshwater and saline lagoons with associated marshland or mangrove swamp are found in the interiors. Tall, wispy casuarinas (an exotic tree species introduced by the Portuguese and planted in order to stabilize the dunes and beaches) are a common feature of the dunes. Otherwise the landscape is sparsely covered with a sprinkling of dune specific scrambler plants, mangroves, broad-leafed woodland and cultivated crops.

It is thought that the islands were originally joined together as one long spit, lying on the seaward side of what was a

A variety of dolphin species occur in the warm waters of the Indian Ocean. The graceful creatures pictured here frolic off the shores of Mozambique.

massive delta, most probably linked to the Limpopo River system. Over many thousands of years they became separated from each other and the mainland by changing sea levels, followed by wind and wave activity eroding the lower lying areas. Of particular interest is the fact that the islands are constantly narrowing and the uncovered dunes, most notably those on Bazaruto Island, are moving in a westward direction. Their exposure to the elements via the prevailing winds and the perpetual erosive action of the sea are slowly taking their toll, highlighting their extremely sensitive make-up and the need for all visitors to be acutely aware that the vegetation cover should not be damaged in any way.

Welcoming visitors to the islands are several established lodges, all offering quality accommodation and a variety of water sports in tropical surroundings. On the very northern tip of Bazaruto Island lies the Pestana Hotels and Resorts-owned Bazaruto Lodge, spread along the water's edge beneath an extensive grove of coconut palms and under the watchful light of the Archipelago's only lighthouse. An intriguing feature of the area, and making for the ultimate sunset walk, is a 4-kilometre-

long (2,5-mile) sand spit gently curving from the front of the lodge into the deep turquoise waters of the open sea. Over the years the lodge's skippers have established an enviable record of landing the 'big one' and are responsible for most of the legendary fishing tales stemming from these waters. Built on an incline towards the southern end of the island and affording spectacular views over the bay towards the mainland, is the Indigo Bay Lodge.

The elegantly rustic Benguerra Lodge, situated on a secluded bay a short distance from the northern point of Benguerra Island, exudes romantic charm. The lodge and its raised chalets are discreetly hidden under an inviting canopy of milkwoods and silver beeches, allowing beach views while enveloped in lush greenery. On the southern side of Benguerra and looking onto Flamingo Bay is the most sizable of the lodges, Marlin Lodge, which is particularly suited for larger groups and boasts conference facilities among its attractions.

Magaruque Lodge is the only resort on Magaruque Island and at the time of writing was undergoing extensive renovations. When visiting any of these lodges, be sure to include an evening

walk up one of the higher sand dunes for a panorama of the ever-changing seascapes at sunset. Santa Carolina once enjoyed the standing of being the premier tropical island getaway in the Indian Ocean, earning the name of 'Paradise Island'.

The waters surrounding the Archipelago offer some of the most exciting and challenging saltwater fishing in Southern Africa. The warm currents of the Mozambique Channel range along the eastern edge of the chain and, together with a fairly steep drop-off in the continental shelf, contribute to creating choice fishing conditions. Traditionally, lure and bait fishing have always been the preferred methods, but growing in popularity is the sport of fly-fishing. For those who have mastered its intricacies, the rewards are the more sought-after species: barracuda, tuna, sailfish, kingfish, mackerel and queenfish. But the biggest prize of all is the majestic marlin, still caught off the islands in reasonable numbers between July and December.

A heartening aspect of the fishing operations run by the lodges is the practice of 'tag and release', increasingly used for the migratory species such as marlin, sailfish and barracuda. Efforts are also afoot to persuade boat skippers and anglers to release fish (Bazaruto Lodge offers financial incentives to its skippers for releasing bill-fish) once the dinner-table catch has been boated.

Those who prefer to spend their leisure time in the water rather than bobbing on its surface are well catered for as the islands offer diving and snorkelling sites that rank among Africa's finest. Names such as the Aquarium and Two-Mile, Five-Mile and Twelve-Mile reefs are world-renowned for their spectacular diving.

The coral reefs are varied with both deep-water and shallow sites, some being as close as 20 metres (65 feet) from the shoreline and no more than a few metres deep. For coral to grow successfully in large colonies, it requires a combination of warm water, extensive sunlight, a stable seabed, low silt levels and high water salinity, conditions which all occur in the waters around the Archipelago. Besides an amazing assortment of tropical and game fish species and the kaleidoscope of corals providing an unforgettable colour feast, divers also have the chance of bumping into one of the six dolphin and five turtle species that occur in the area. The ultimate underwater encounter is with either the inquisitive manta ray or the giant whale shark, both impressive in size, yet harmless to man.

Unbeknown to many visitors is the wealth of interesting and unusual wildlife that lives on and around the islands. In an effort to protect their sensitive ecosystems, the islands of Magaruque, Benguerra and Bangue were declared a national park in 1971. Bazaruto Island and Santa Carolina have not yet been included in the park, although their status as such is awaiting ratification.

The most intriguing of the animals found in the area is the highly endangered *sirenian*, the dugong. Often referred to as 'seacows' or 'mermaids', these large (they can reach lengths of over 3 metres [10 feet] and weigh more than 350 kilograms [772 pounds]),

blubbery, herbivorous marine mammals are found in the coastal waters of the Indian and Pacific oceans.

The coast of Mozambique is their recognized southernmost range in Africa, with Bazaruto being one of the very few localities where they occur in reasonable numbers. Sadly, recent aerial surveys have indicated an alarming decline in their population, possibly suggesting that within the next decade, they may become extinct in Mozambique's waters. In 1993, surveys accounted for only about 110 dugongs, already warning of the threat to the animal's survival, while the most recent survey, conducted in 1997, accounted for no more than 15, which does not constitute a viable population.

Other animals of interest are the suni, red duiker, bushbuck, samango monkey and red squirrel, and the freshwater crocodiles that occur in the inland lakes on Bazaruto and Benguerra. There are 45 recorded species of amphibians and reptiles, including four endemic lizards, and over 145 bird species. A highlight for bird-watchers is the rich diversity of waders and seabirds, and for those who visit in the winter months there is an opportunity to witness the flocks of flamingos that feed along the tidal shallows on the western sides of Bazaruto, Benguerra and Magaruque.

THE BEIRA CORRIDOR

Encompassing a narrow stretch of land that extends from the coastal city of Beira in the east to the country's border with Zimbabwe in the west, the Beira Corridor includes the towns of Dondo, Gondola, Inchope, Chimoio, Bandula and Manica, all lying along the Corridor's main route. Beira, often referred to as the 'heart of Mozambique' because of its central location, is the country's second-largest city with a population close on 400,000 people.

A grimy port city situated at the mouth of the Pũngoè River, Beira is also the economic and administrative hub of Mozambique's interior. Botswana, Zimbabwe, Zambia and Malawi, all land-locked countries, make use of the port as an export-import window to the outside world. The 'corridor' vision is based on a long-term economic development plan that incorporates the upgrading of the port facilities, road and rail links inland, telecommunications and the supporting service industries that will encourage increased use of the port by Mozambique's neighbours.

Although having strategic importance, the city itself is impoverished and run down, and in dire need of rejuvenation – the infrastructure, city centre and suburbs are all suffering from the many years of turmoil and neglect. Situated 1,262 kilometres (785 miles) from Maputo, Beira has become a stronghold for the opposition RENAMO party (Resistencia Naçional de Moçambique, or the National Resistance of Mozambique).

The original town was known as Sofala and was used by the Arabs as a trading post before the Portuguese elected it to become their first settlement in East Africa in 1505. It was built on the southern side of Beira Bay but no longer exists as the sea has since claimed the last remnants. Present-day Beira's site

Most of Mozambique's coastal resorts boast first class and easily accessible snorkelling sites.

was reputed to have been chosen by the British who were instrumental in initiating the building of the port and railway line in 1897–98 to serve their economic interests in Rhodesia (now Zimbabwe). The fact that it was built on and around swampy land, with parts of the city lying below sea-level, was presumably disregarded, an oversight that makes today's Beira an extremely difficult and expensive city to maintain.

The Portuguese colonial government developed an ingenious system of interlinked canals and pump stations that proved very efficient in controlling tidal waters as well as excess rain and sewage water, but since independence this system has fallen into disrepair and is no longer effective. Walking the streets is an exercise in avoiding piles of waste material, while driving is no easier as the roads are hazardous, and the constant hustling attention by hundreds of poverty-stricken street children can be tiring. If you do visit the city, be sure to stay at the Hotel Embaixador with its cosy pub. The hotel's owner, Francisco Brandão, a second-generation Portuguese Mozambican, offers a wealth of information and historical facts about the city and surrounding areas, and his family history also makes for fascinating listening.

Mozambique's best-known and most accessible park, Gorongosa National Park, lies in the central region of Sofala Province, 70 kilometres (45 miles) north of Inchope on the main Beira/Zimbabwe highway. Its reputation for abundant game, particularly lion, buffalo and elephant, was gained prior to independence when large numbers of visitors filled the park's base camp, Chitengo. First established in 1920 as a hunting area, the park was upgraded in 1940 to a game reserve and again in 1960 to a national park. Gorongosa's boundaries lie on the higher edges of the Urema drainage basin, part of the southern limit of the Great East African Rift Valley, and includes the large wetland area in its lower lying central regions known as Urema Lake.

The Cahora Bassa Dam wall. The name is apparently derived from the Chewa phrase kebrabassa, *meaning 'the work is over'.*

Although no longer able to offer visitors the resort atmosphere and game-viewing spectacle of its heyday, the park remains an exciting destination for birders and botanists and those seeking tranquil surroundings. The future of the park is in the very capable hands of one of the wildlife department's most passionate and visionary conservationists, Roberto Zolho. He has assembled a team of anti-poaching scouts and community guards who have committed themselves to rehabilitating Gorongosa and its wildlife populations. A major part of their work is focussed in involving the surrounding communities through education projects, employment and establishing sustainable local economies.

The western half of the Beira Corridor runs through Manica Province. Situated just short of the Zimbabwean border is the small and interesting Manica Town. Lying among the mountains of the Vumba range, Manica has a long and colourful history associated with small-scale mining and prospecting. The Arabs, the first to exploit the area for gold, were known to have had a 'gold route' linking the town to the coast. The Portuguese, through the efforts of the 'Companhia de Moçambique', began prospecting for gold, silver and copper in the late 1800s, and by the early 1900s had established numerous small but viable mining operations. This was in spite of an attempt by Cecil John Rhodes and the then British South Africa Police to annex the area because of its mineral wealth.

Although the larger commercial mines ceased operating years ago, many of the valleys in the surrounding mountains are still being excavated by groups of local gold diggers. Under what would seem to be fairly treacherous conditions, these prospectors dig pits of up to 16 metres (52 feet) deep into the bowels of the earth before the recovered orange soils are panned in the many clear streams that spring from the hills.

From Manica, the main road leaving Mozambique and heading for Zimbabwe leads to the Great Eastern Escarpment. This highland region serves as the catchment area for eight river systems, the major ones being the Messica, Revue and Nyamangena rivers, all flowing into the Chicamba Real Dam. Weary travellers using the corridor route to and from Zimbabwe will find a little oasis 44 kilometres (27 miles) from the border on the shores of Chicamba. Casa Msika offers comfortable chalets, a swimming pool and a good restaurant overlooking the tranquil waters of the dam, and for those who are keen fishermen, the chance to cast a line for bass and tilapia.

TETE AND CAHORA BASSA DAM

The most significant aspect of Tete Province is the fact that it is home to Africa's third-largest hydroelectric power station and the Cahora Bassa Dam, situated on the Zambezi River. Built by a consortium using South African, Portuguese and European funding and expertise, the project has always attracted its fair share of controversy as certain quarters questioned who would benefit from the scheme and at what cost to Mozambique. Issues came to a head when Mozambique gained independence and the FRELIMO (Frente de Libertaçao de Moçambique, or the Liberation Front of Mozambique) government refused to accept responsibility for the capital and maintenance costs of the venture. Presently, the Portuguese government is liable to complete the payments on the project, after which Cahora Bassa reverts to full Mozambican ownership.

Although the station's five generators have a 4,000-megawatt potential, sufficient to supply all of Mozambique and

some of South Africa and Zimbabwe's power needs, they have never reached anything near full capacity and at present only supply power to the local districts of Songo and Tete. It is planned, however, to have the power station operating on a profit basis by the year 2000.

Construction on the project began in 1969 and it was not until 1974 that the dam started filling up, creating an enormous lake that now stretches, 270 kilometres (168 miles) in length, from the dam wall at Songo in the east to the border town of Zumbo in the west, and is up to140 metres (460 feet) deep. In the process Cahora Bassa acquired its very own 'lost town', and with it legends of rich deposits of silver beneath the dam's shimmering surface. The administrative town of Chicoa became submerged with the rising waters, the government having to evacuate its residents to higher ground. The dam wall, 171 metres (560 feet) high above the foundations, holds back over 52,000 million cubic metres (68,009 million cubic yards) of water which covers an area of approximately2,660 square kilometres (1,027 square miles).

The dam may not be fulfilling its primary function at the moment, but certainly is providing fertile grounds for a thriving kapenta-fishing industry. What used to be known as Lake Tanganyika sardines (*Limnothrissa miodon*) found their way into the dam via the Zambezi River from Lake Kariba in Zimbabwe. The kapenta industry on Cahora Bassa is relatively new with the first operators putting rigs onto the water in 1994, but has since expanded into a respectable income source, providing employment for close on 2,000 fisherman. The dozens of protected bays and inlets in and around the area known as Chicoa, 50 kilometres (30 miles) from the dam wall, harbour the land operations of the various companies.

Sunset heralds the arrival of the many kapenta rigs operating on the dam's open waters. With the aid of strong lighting, the kapenta are caught at night by lowering large circular nets up to 30 metres

(100 feet) into the water. A good night's fishing may see a single rig arriving at the drying racks in the morning with up to three tons of fish on board. The salted and dried product ends up in 25-kilogram (55-pound) sacks, to be transported and sold to the markets of Mozambique, Zambia, Malawi and Zimbabwe.

Presently, two low-key camps at Cahora Bassa offer fishing and birding excursions. Ugezi Tiger Lodge is situated a short distance from the dam wall, providing guests fishing opportunities in the shadows of the lofty cliffs that make up the Zambezi Gorge. Camanga Resort has more serene surroundings above the gorge where the dam is at its most expansive. Fishing for tigerfish, bream and chessa along the dam's tranquil edges is a pleasing way to pass the time.

In years to come, Cahora Bassa will surely grow to match southern Africa's prime freshwater fishing destinations. That a pristine expanse of waters this size and in such an awesome setting still exists as an untouched wilderness is a minor wonder. If it is not to follow the lazy flight of one of the many fish eagles or goliath herons, then it is the rugged vista of the distant mountain ranges that hold your attention. Like so many of the natural treasures in Mozambique, the sense of complete solitude and tranquillity is the main appeal.

The dusty city of Tete straddles the Zambezi River about 120 kilometres (75 miles) downstream of the dam wall where the wide floodplains allow the river to broaden, slowing its flow. The sluggish pace of the river as it passes calmly through Tete belies its force, something that may well have occurred to David Livingstone some 140 years ago. It was from here that he led two unsuccessful expeditions upstream in an attempt to ascend the raging waters of the Quebrabasa Rapids.

Because of its strategic position, equidistant from the borders of Malawi and Zimbabwe, and being Mozambique's only reliable crossing point over the river, Tete has a bustling atmosphere with a

A coconut palm plantation on the idyllic island of Quirambas, which forms part of Cabo Delgado Province.

constant flow of traffic passing through. During the war years the Malawi to Zimbabwe route through Tete remained one of the few busy roads, even though the traffic often had to make use of military convoys for protection. Taking the dirt road north for 30 kilometres (20 miles) and following the edge of the Zambezi's southern bank, the gracious grounds of the Jesuit mission station of Boroma are reached. Built in 1890, the ancient church and surrounding mission are now used as an educational centre by the local authorities.

QUELIMANE AND SURROUNDS

The name Quelimane is derived from the Chuabo word *quolimane*, and refers to the manual tasks that need to be performed in preparing the fields for planting. An apt choice for the capital city of Zambezia Province indeed, as the region's low-lying swamplands are exceedingly fertile and the majority of its citizens are involved in the agricultural sector in some way. Approaching the city from the inland town of Nicoadala, the

intensity of and the variations in the colour green are striking. Massive commercial coconut plantations extend as far as the eye can see, while rice, maize, sugar cane and banana and mango trees jostle for the remaining space not soaked by the tidal waters of the Rio dos Boas Sinais (the River of Good Omens). The river was so named by Vasco da Gama who stopped at Quelimane on his first trip to India in order to restock with food and allow his crew time to recover from scurvy. It is reputed that on receiving news that he could find a navigator who would be able to show him the way to the East, he named the river as an omen of his good fortune.

Situated approximately 20 kilometres (12,5 miles) from the sea, Quelimane is enveloped on three sides by the river's interlinked system of channels, tidal estuaries and mangrove swamps. Many of the city's poorer citizens have made their homes on the scant portions of remaining land among these tidal flats and between the coconut and mangrove trees surrounding the established

city centre, creating a patchwork of densely populated suburbs and markets on its outskirts.

Quelimane, designated a city in 1544, was one of the earliest Portuguese settlements, and today has a population of approximately 300,000. It was originally started as a port to serve the needs of the tea, cashew nut, coconut, cotton and sugar industries. The port also played an important role for the Portuguese at the height of the slave trade as it was at the end of the Zambezi route, one of the busiest in the region. Today, Quelimane carries on its agricultural traditions and remains an important port for the industry.

It is also the agricultural headquarters for one of Mozambique's largest industrial corporations, Grupo Madal. Founded in 1903, the group has built up a diversified portfolio of business interests that includes timber, cattle and game ranching, fishing, salt, shipping and commercial trading. The largest of its interests, coconut and copra production, is situated in and around Quelimane with the group owning over 27,000 hectares (66,733 acres) of coconut trees and about 30 per cent of the country's total production under cultivation, making it the leader in this field.

Travellers heading to the northern regions of Mozambique are likely to make use of Quelimane as a stopover point, as it is the first major city after crossing the Zambezi via Caia or traversing Malawi via Tete. The Hotel Chuabo, often referred to by locals as the 'best hotel outside of Maputo', offers clean, comfortable rooms and good food. The owners of the hotel pride themselves on the fact that, in the darkest days of the war, they still managed to serve a tasty and varied menu to locals and travellers alike, despite food rationing.

Praia de Zalala, hidden among coconut and casuarina trees roughly 45 kilometres (28 miles) from Quelimane, offers a quieter alternative to the bustle of the city. Its wide, white beaches have for many years been a choice destination for the wealthier Quelimane and Beira set.

Just over 100 kilometres (62 miles) south of Quelimane is the mouth of the Zambezi River, where its muddy waters

This lovely Makua woman comes from the country's northern regions.

are fanned out by a large delta before spilling into the Indian Ocean. The core of the delta is a swampy wetland of channels bordered by papyrus beds and palm and evergreen forests, with mangrove trees lining the estuary. Since the construction of Lake Kariba and Cahora Bassa, the river's annual floodwaters are

withheld, dramatically reducing the levels of water and silt entering the delta. The result has been a gradual change in the delta's shape and composition, allowing invasive vegetation species to penetrate the alluvial grasslands, and channels to become blocked.

The Marromeu Buffalo Reserve lies on the southern bank of the Zambezi Delta and has three river systems crossing its luxuriant plains, all originating on the Cheringoma Plateau to the west, before they flow into the greater delta system. The reserve offers a refuge of wetland and forest mix to its dwindling game populations which at one time consisted of over 30,000 buffalo and carried healthy herds of elephant, hippo and sable. The alarming decline in numbers has been the result of intense commercial and trophy hunting pressure, and the slaughter that took place during and immediately after the war, leaving only a few thousand buffalo and scattered pockets of various antelope species, such as bushbuck, waterbuck and reedbuck.

NAMPULA AND ILHA DE MOÇAMBIQUE

Roughly 200 kilometres (125 miles) from the coast and surrounded by a fortress of granite inselbergs lies Nampula, the metropolis of the north. Before the Portuguese settled here, the region was known as M'pula, after a Makua chief who once ruled the area. The city serves as the commercial and administrative centre for government as well as the extensive agricultural interests of the major companies in the northern provinces. Other than the enormous twin-towered cathedral in the centre of town, one of the finest in Mozambique, and the National Museum, the city is unspectacular in its historical and cultural offerings. For those visiting Nampula, the Hotel Tropical offers comfortable lodging in the shady confines of some extremely large fig trees.

Nampula is the link between the port of Nacala to the east and Malawi to the west, in what is known as the Nacala

A woman from Vunduzi prepares maize and vegetables for the evening meal.

A dense concentration of palm trees flanks the coastline around Palma in northeastern Mozambique.

Corridor. Perched on a hillside and overlooking the town's deep-water harbour, Nacala is a relatively clean and tidy port town. It serves as the major outlet for exports from Malawi, Zambia and the northern regions of Mozambique. Around the corner from the sheltered bay, local fishermen ply the shallower azure waters of Fernão Veloso. This area offers one of the few easily accessible and secluded beach destinations in the north.

Not as accessible, but worth the effort of driving the 180 kilometres (110 miles) on reasonable gravel road from Nampula, is the coastal town of Angoche. First impressions gained are of a town surviving as a shell of its pre-independence prominence. Evidence of it having been a boom town is unmistakable, with incomplete buildings as well as abandoned factories and warehouses in abundance. It is not for these relics that you visit Angoche, however, but for the endless, unspoiled and immaculately clean beaches that lie a short distance from the town.

Completing the Nacala Corridor is the road leading west from Nampula via Cuamba and onto Malawi, arguably the most scenically satisfying section of countryside Mozambique has to offer. If driven during the late summer months, this route offers a breathtaking combination of monolithic inselberg formations, many looming dramatically close to the roadside, and an endless patchwork of croplands, palm groves and indigenous woodland splashed in lush greens and yellows. Villages and towns hug the gravel road the full distance, providing the ultimate in rural African trips.

If you had to visit a single destination in Mozambique to experience the country's cosmopolitan mix, it would have to be Ilha de Moçambique, an enthralling microcosm on an island a mere 2,5 kilometres (1,5 miles) long and 600 metres (1,969 feet) wide. On this postage stamp-sized crop of ancient coral rock, somehow nearly 12,000 people have managed to cram themselves on to it. Access is limited to light motor vehicles able to squeeze between the

posts erected on either side of the 3,5-kilometre-long (2,2-mile) single-lane bridge built in the 1960s, linking the island to the mainland, or what the locals refer to as the 'continent'.

Centuries before Vasco da Gama first arrived in 1498, the Arabs had established on the island a busy trading post and in the process, spread the religion of Islam and many of their customs among the local Bantu-speaking peoples. In 1507 the Portuguese occupied the island in order to defend their trading interests, and as a strategic stopover on the route to Goa. By the latter part of the century they had established the colossal fort of St Sebastião on the northern side (construction began in 1554 and was only completed decades later), built around the church of Nossa Senhora do Baluarte, and the fort of St Lourenço (1588) on a tiny coral outcrop on the southern side. It was not the Arabs or the Indians that posed the severest threat to the Portuguese, but rather the Dutch who attacked the island three times in the early 1600s. They ransacked the place twice, burning the cathedrals and chapels, but were never able to unseat the defending soldiers from the forts and eventually conceded that it was Portuguese territory.

For the next two centuries Ilha de Moçambique became the centre of Portuguese interests along the east coast and was the 'capital city' until 1898, when the seat of governor was moved to then Lourenço Marques, and the regional capital until 1935 when that was moved to Nampula. The high population statistic is a recent phenomenon that began during the war years as people from the mainland sought safety from the conflict on the island. Those who were unable to find shelter on the northern side, in Stonetown and among the old colonial homes abandoned by the Portuguese at independence, set up residence on the southern side in the more heavily populated and poorer section known as Macuti.

Today the citizens, who are predominantly of the Makua group, go about their leisurely existence surrounded by the heritage of a turbulent history, allowing visitors glimpses of the rich cultural influences that have impacted on their lives.

A Makua painted face is for adornment and indicates the woman's coming of age.

The island should not be sought out as a beach destination, as the high number of residents has ensured that its shores and surrounding waters are not the cleanest. To enjoy swimming and snorkelling in the area, hop the short distance by boat to Ilha das Cobras or Goa Island.

PEMBA AND THE NORTH

The city of Pemba, known as Porto Amelia during the Portuguese period, serves as the major fishing and timber port for the region. Situated on a promontory at the narrow entrance to Pemba Bay, reputed by the locals to be one of the world's largest natural bays, the city began its history as an important Arab slave-trading port. So busy was the port that its Makua name was derived from its descriptive meaning 'the boats afloat on the water', in reference to the many slave ships moored here. Today, Pemba is more comfortable with its present reputation of being a favourite holiday destination, especially for Mozambicans and Portuguese visitors, and its palm-lined silvery beach, Praia de Wimbe, lies only 3 kilometres (2 miles) from the city centre. The Wimbe beachfront is dominated by the Complexo Turístico Naútilus comprising several bungalows, numerous self-contained units and a large restaurant patio affording pleasant sea views.

North of Pemba and extending all the way up to the mouth of the Rovuma River, Mozambique's northern border with Tanzania, is the chain of 32 islands known as the Quirimbas Archipelago. Other than the three largest islands of Matemo, Ibo and Quirimbas, the rest do not have permanent populations, as their coral rock foundations hold no fresh

Early morning fishing in the shallows at Praia da Wimbe, Pemba. The area is one of Mozambique's most beautiful.

water. Gaining access to the islands can be a formidable task as the 10-kilometre-stretch (6-mile) separating them from the mainland is a maze of mangrove swamps and tidal flats, making successful boat crossings dependant on having an accomplished dhow skipper. Ibo was the region's major port until the early 1930s when that distinction moved to Pemba because of its superior harbour facilities.

Now supporting only a small fishing community, Ibo's southern half has a 'ghost-town' feel to it as the islanders go about their daily lives among the abandoned and decaying administrative and port buildings of yesteryear. The more southerly island of Quirimbas is synonymous with the Gessner Family whose roots on the island go back to 1928 when Frederich Gessner first settled on its shores. Today, his son, Joachim and wife Sieglinde own a 65,000-tree coconut plantation and a large herd of cattle, and look after visitors staying at their guest houses. When visiting these islands, it is a good idea to

stay with the Gessners and walk the 4 kilometres (2,5 miles) to Ibo at low tide through the fascinating labyrinth of mangrove channels, returning on the incoming tide.

Further north lie the picturesque palm-wreathed fishing villages of Pangane and Palma. Remote in their subtropical setting, the folk conduct their day-to-day living in a timeless fashion. The dirty port town of Mocímboa da Praia, the last potential fuel stop before the northern border, lies between the two.

To the west and moving inland, the Mueda plateau is the homeland of the proud Makonde people. The modest town of Mueda is the largest urban area, resting high on the plateau in apparent isolation from the remainder of the country, its altitude providing a refreshing interlude from the humidity of the coastal strip. The fiercely independent Makonde people give the impression that they would prefer to be left to their traditional devices, some of which have achieved celebrated status. Makonde

carvings, usually hewn from heavy black ebony, are intricate and ornate, and often depict their beliefs.

The Makonde are also passionate followers of ceremony and rituals, most often performed by masked dancers known as *mapicos* and accompanied by a throng of drummers. Although reverent in their execution, the colourful *mapicos* often introduce a note of humour and festivity into the sequence of dances and it is not unusual for them to wear masks that portray the comical side of life.

Any visit to the northern regions is not complete without undertaking the arduous, yet captivating trek into the hinterlands of Niassa Province in search of one of Mozambique's finest wilderness areas, the Niassa Reserve. The route to the reserve runs westwards, slipping through the farming town of Montepuez in Cabo Delgado and along a seemingly endless dirt track that winds its way to Marrupa. It then swings north for another daunting 150 kilometres (95 miles) before reaching the distant village of Mercula, the

Elephant lumber through the dense undergrowth of the Niassa Reserve, one of the few reserves that carries substantial numbers of game.

headquarters of the Niassa Reserve Project. This enterprising project is a joint venture between the national government, private investors and the local communities, and is aimed at safeguarding one of Africa's last remaining true wilderness areas while enhancing the quality of life for the surrounding communities.

Covering 35,000 square kilometres (13,514 square miles) between the northern boundary of the Rovuma River and the southern boundary of the Lugenda River, the greater extent of the reserve will include a number of rural settlements, designated the Multiple Resource Utilization Area, and a buffer zone comprising five hunting blocks around the perimeter of the wilderness zone.

Niassa holds the largest numbers of Mozambique's remaining wildlife with reasonable populations of elephant, buffalo, sable, eland, lion and leopard, and has the distinction of being the home range for a variety of rare and endemic subspecies. Roaming the reserve's undulating plains, predominantly covered with brachystegia woodland and grassland savanna, and commanded over by some exceptionally spectacular inselberg formations, are the last herds of Niassa wildebeest (*Connochaetes taurinus* subsp. *johnstonii*) and Johnston's impala (*Aepyceros melampus* subsp. *johnstonii*). A subspecies of Burchell's zebra and waterbuck have also been reported in the reserve.

THE WILDERNESS AREAS

One of Mozambique's mysteries is that the true condition of its wilderness areas and the numbers of its wildlife populations are unknown. No individual or department seems to have an accurate record of species counts or the status of the environments in which the various species occur. This has been compounded by the fact that the majority of the designated wilderness areas are in remote regions of the country, fairly

inaccessible to the average traveller and demanding and costly to monitor by the authorities. The sad reality is that the wildlife populations have been dramatically reduced, and that the environments in which they occur were badly neglected during the many years of civil conflict.

But Mozambique is blessed with a diverse array of ecosystems, and magnificent land- and seascapes. Vast tracts of coastal marshland, mangrove swamps and dune forests extend into lowland

Paul Dutton and Spirit of the Wilderness *take a well-earned rest from doing aerial dugong counts.*

grassland savanna and dry forest through mid-altitude miombo woodland and riverine forest, and then up to the highland subtropical and tropical forests.

It is these lands that once did, and could again in the future, support great numbers of animals on its plains and in its forests. The decimation of animal life was the result of continual meat hunting by colonial and local armies, and wholesale commercial ivory poaching by citizens and bandits, resulting in species counts in many areas dropping to zero. Those pockets of elephant, buffalo, hippo and various antelope and predator species that survived, did so in small and isolated populations.

The conflicts have ceased, but left the twin legacies of a displaced population and under-development, as well as insufficient structures to cope with wildlife

management; new and no less serious threats to the country's wilderness areas have thus arisen. In the people's scramble to resettle land, feed themselves and begin small cash economies, the pressures on wildlife and its habitats continue to be substantial. Large areas, particularly in the central and northern provinces, are threatened by 'slash-and-burn' subsistence farmers, and commercial and meat poaching is still pervasive. Considerable activity in illegal and uncontrolled logging is taking place without regard for the sustainability of the resources, and indiscriminate and exploitative trophy hunters are taking advantage of the poor licensing systems, while the coastline is jeopardized by ever-increasing numbers of visitors without the necessary environmental safeguards.

Fortunately, the outlook is not only one of gloom as, since 1992, the government and numerous private individuals and organizations have been involved in a multitude of projects aimed at reclaiming and rehabilitating the national parks and wilderness areas to their former status. Since these projects began, the decline in some species, notably elephant and buffalo, has been halted, thanks largely to certain visionary and industrious members of the Directorate of National Forests and Wildlife (DNFFB), and the invaluable work done by non-government organizations (NGOs) such as the Endangered Wildlife Trust, the World Bank and the Convention on International Trade in Endangered Species (CITES).

Driven by passion and extreme commitment to the plight of the environment is Paul Dutton, who has been involved in conservation and research in Mozambique for the last 30 years. His work on the Bazaruto Archipelago and in Gorongosa National Park has been invaluable, and he has been involved in species counts in most of the wilderness areas, constantly informing the government and private sector about the need for sound environmental management.

Mozambique's wilderness areas are classified as national parks, game reserves, controlled hunting areas and forest reserves. To date, 78,842 square kilometres (3,414 square miles), representing 9.7 per cent of the total land surface, have been proclaimed as one of the above. The four national parks are Gorongosa in Sofala Province (5,370 square kilometres; 2,073 square miles); Banhine in Gaza Province (7,000 square kilometres; 2,703 square miles); Zinave in Inhambane Province (3,700 square kilometres; 1,429 square miles), and Bazaruto, offshore from Inhambane Province (150 square kilometres; 58 square miles). The five game reserves are Niassa Reserve in Niassa Province (presently 15,000 square kilometres [5,792 square miles] but proposed to be increased to 22,000 square kilometres [8,495 square miles]); Gile Reserve in Zambezia Province (2,100 square kilometres; 810 square miles); Marromeu Buffalo Reserve in Sofala Province (1,500 square kilometres; 579 square miles); Maputo Elephant Reserve in Maputo Province (700 square kilometres; 270 square miles), and Pomene Reserve in Inhambane Province (200 square kilometres; 77 square miles).

The thirteen controlled hunting areas, known as *coutadas*, range in size from just over 1,000 square kilometres (386 square miles) to the largest, Coutada 16, at 10,000 square kilometres (3,861 square miles) along the border with South Africa's Kruger National Park. The *coutadas* are presently held on short leases by hunting operators, but plans are in the pipeline to improve their profile within the country's wildlife portfolio. A further two per cent of the land holds the status of 'special protection area' or 'wildlife production unit'. These tracts await legislation as to whether they will become controlled hunting areas, private game concessions or will be integrated into existing national parks and reserves.

The country has seventeen forest reserves totalling an area of about 4,500 square kilometres (1,738 square miles), the majority situated in the provinces of Maputo, Nampula, Manica and Sofala. Gaza and Zambezia provinces each only have one forest reserve.

The areas of Banhine, Zinhave and Coutada 16 are Mozambique's potential contribution to the bold trilateral plan to create a mega-reserve, unofficially known as the Trans Frontier Conservation Area, that proposes to include South Africa's eastern edge of the Kruger National Park and Zimbawe's Gonarezhou National Park. This audacious attempt at cross-border conservation has been six years in planning, and has been funded to date by the World Bank, the respective countries' wildlife bodies, and a handful of private patrons. The planned next phase is to concession out areas in-between the proclaimed reserves with the idea that the private concession holders will be responsible for restocking the game in their respective areas and in time to incorporate all into one large reserve.

The best options to view and photograph game in Mozambique are at the Maputo Elephant Reserve, Gorongosa National Park and the Niassa Reserve. Most of the remaining areas are difficult to access or suffer from a lack of infrastructure. It will require time and funding before the country re-establishes a fully developed network of wilderness options. Because of the small number of people who venture into these Edens, anyone who takes the trouble and a reliable four-wheel-drive will experience the ultimate safari away from the masses who visit the better-known destinations in Southern and East Africa.

HISTORY

PRE-COLONIAL
Archaeological finds indicate that the first-known people to have inhabited what is present-day Mozambique were hunter-gatherers and pastoralists,

around 4000 B.C. The first Bantu-speaking populations began migrating from Central and East Africa during the first century A.D. and by the 10th century were firmly settled, living as agriculturists and traders in clan and tribal groups under chieftainships and kings. The most powerful of these were the Karanga dynasties whose empire was centred around Great Zimbabwe and later the kingdom of Mwenamutapa, both of whose rule extended to the coastal regions of central Mozambique and into the highlands of Malawi.

Coinciding with this inland movement, the Arab empires began extending their spheres of influence on the African continent during the 9th and 10th centuries, opening up new trading routes and establishing strongholds on the coast. By the 12th century, the Arabs had created trading centres all along the East African coastline, stretching from Somalia as far south as Sofala (today known as Beira). Many of these centres – among them Malindi, Zanzibar, Mafia, Mozambique Island and Sofala – grew into port cities with a strong African/Arabic cultural and religious identity, and were mainly involved with trading between the empires of the Persian Gulf, southeast Asia and the African hinterland.

The Arabs brought clay pottery, ceramics, spices, weapons and intricate jewellery in exchange for slaves, ivory, gold and other metals. They also introduced a variety of crops and fruits including rice, citrus, sugar cane, coconut, banana and mango. In modern Mozambique Arabic influences are very much a part of the country's history, architecture and culture, with the northern coastal regions having a large Muslim population.

THE ARRIVAL OF THE PORTUGUESE
In 1498 the Portuguese navigator and explorer, Vasco da Gama, sailed around the southern tip of Africa en route to India. It was on this journey that he staked Portugal's future claim to Mozambique when he stopped off at Inhambane, Quelimane and Ilha de Moçambique. It

took another 100 years before Portugal had established the territory as a part of their Crown land by means of a mixture of military power, diplomacy and trading influence. Their major concern was to wrest control of the local and Indian Ocean trade routes from the Arabs, in order to maximize their gain in dealing in the area's products, especially gold, silver and ivory. However, as Portugal was one of Europe's poorest states with a local economy based mostly on wine and olives, the country found it increasingly difficult to maintain its influence and penetrate further inland from its coastal settlements and trading posts.

In the early 1600s the Portuguese Crown attempted to overcome this situation by granting vast tracts of land to established Portuguese settlers. These Afro-Portuguese, or *muzungos*, were entrusted with establishing their estates (known as *prazos)* as commercial and agricultural enterprises, thereby expanding and protecting Portuguese sovereignty. Most of these estates were set up in the Zambezi Valley and the lowland plains inland of Sofala. In exchange, the *prazo* owners would help to exert the government's influence by collecting local taxes and looking after Portuguese troops stationed in their areas. In 1752, the Portuguese Crown took a further step to consolidate control over the territory by moving authority away from Portuguese India (Goa) and placing it directly under the influence of Lisbon. Although the *prazo* system was partially successful over a period of 300 years (it was outlawed in the 1930s), it always remained fractious due to the continual disputes between the Portuguese authorities and local African leaders. On introduction of the system, the *prazo* owners were entitled to engage in the trading of slaves, which they did to the system's eventual detriment; over time, a further problem was the scarcity of able manpower to work the fields. Although the government attempted to eliminate slavery in 1836, the practice was so well-entrenched and profitable that the decrees were ignored.

The late Samora Machel, the country's first independently elected president.

The middle and latter parts of the 19th century saw the strengthening of British, French and South African commercial interests in southeastern Africa. Coinciding with an upsurge in war and revolt by local African leaders, the Portuguese government's hold on Mozambique became even more tenuous. To help consolidate their control, they sold the first charter in 1891 to international business, known as the Companhia de Moçambique, giving them the right to develop and exploit large areas of land. In the following two years they granted similar charters to the Companhia da Zambezia and the Companhia do Niassa.

THE COLONIAL ERA

Portugal gained international acceptance to its claim as the colonial power over Mozambique in a treaty signed in May 1891 between Portugal and Great Britain. This took place seven years after the Berlin Conference, which had dealt

with the claims of the European powers that competed for Africa's land and natural resources. During the previous decade the two powers had been involved in numerous regional treaties before they settled on the boundaries which today make up the Republic of Mozambique. It took another three decades of bloody conflict with the African people before the Portuguese government managed to gain full control and authority within their newly defined international boundaries.

This provided the spur for Lisbon to move control of the country to Mozambique itself by appointing a governor and the first Legislative Council in 1920. What followed was a period of notoriously oppressive rule based on a system of forced labour, known as *chibalo*. This harsh system was formulated on the colonial assumption that all peasant and subsistence farmers were idle, and therefore had a moral obligation to work for the government. Used predominantly for state projects involving agriculture, road works and construction, it was often used by the private sector too, and was only phased out in the early 1960s. Although subjected to a stringent tax system, the local people enjoyed minimal political rights and the Portuguese provided little or no services, compounding their misfortune. The Catholic missionaries, who were the principal providers of education and health, undertook that function.

In 1926 a coup d'état involving both civilian and military authorities took place in Portugal, bringing to power a right wing bloc under the control of Antonio Salazar. They approached the colonial issue with a strong nationalistic fervour, embarking on a purposeful policy of integrating the African people of Mozambique, and the territory, into the stable of Portuguese-speaking countries, preferring to refer to the colonies as 'provinces' of Portugal. Tens of thousands of Portuguese citizens were sent to Mozambique to settle, with the government providing numerous financial

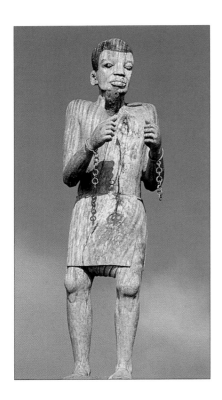

This statue in Mueda commemorates the beginning of the war for independence.

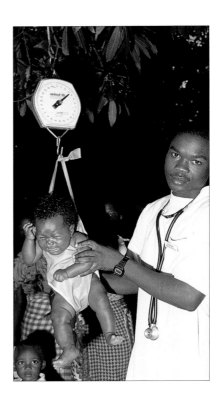

Outdoor mobile clinics are used in the interim while hospitals are being rebuilt.

incentives and social benefits to those who went. Rather than bringing much needed skills and capital, the majority of settlers were unskilled labourers from the lower income brackets. The new government fortified the closer ties by passing the Colonial Act of 1933, legislation that saw Mozambique as a part of Portugal, under a common law and a centrally planned economy.

After the Second World War, the pace of progress picked up with the importation of capital and skills (mainly from Portugal and South Africa) that were needed to broaden the infrastructure and keep Mozambique abreast with the pace of its fellow colonial partners in Africa. It was during this period that a degenerative pattern of development became entrenched, which would later lead to the undoing of Portugal's control.

Mozambique was viewed only as a supplier of food, metals and timber for export back to Portugal with no benefits to the local economy. Local citizens enjoyed no political rights, although the laws of the country were supposedly non-racial. The government's economic and political agenda was linked to its white neighbours, South Africa and the former Rhodesia. These countries were given favoured status with regard to usage of Mozambique's two major ports, Beira and Lourenço Marques, and the mining industry in South Africa used Mozambique as a pool for drawing cheap labour.

The early 1950s saw the beginning of organized resistance to colonial power, taking the form of strike action, rallies and calls by opposition leaders and intellectuals for independence. Despite decolonization taking place all around them, the Portuguese government's resolve to hold on to their colony was brought home with brutal and violent consequences when, on 16 June 1960, police opened fire on thousands of petitioning workers in the northern town of Mueda. This action was a clear signal to the liberation movements and the world that Portugal was prepared to shed blood in order to keep control. Soon after, the government sponsored a second wave of settler immigrants and even enlisted the help of the Catholic Church in order to justify colonialism.

At the instigation of the then Tanzanian president, Julius Nyerere, Mozambique's three anti-colonial groups formed a single independence movement in Dar es Salaam on 25 June 1962. The movement, known as the Frente de Libertaçao de Mocambique (FRELIMO), held its first party congress in September 1962 and elected the non-aligned Eduardo Chivambo Mondlane as its first president.

United by the common goal of seeking an end to colonialism, the organization set out to achieve this by non-violent means and negotiation. Another vicious attack by the government's police on striking workers, this time dockers in Lourenço Marques, persuaded FRELIMO that armed struggle was going to be the only solution. After an initial two-year period of passive resistance against the Portuguese government, FRELIMO launched its armed struggle for independence in September 1964, the first strike taking place in Cabo Delgado Province.

Although world opinion at the time was firmly sided with the liberation movements in Africa, the Portuguese government chose to ignore United Nation's resolutions and pressure, banking on the fact that the world body had no power to implement them. Also, Portugal received tacit support from the Western super powers and South Africa, with none of them coming out in favour of the liberation movements. It was clear to FRELIMO that, although their plight was world news, the slow process of international politics was not going to solve Mozambique's standoff and that the armed struggle would have to be intensified. The next ten years saw the FRELIMO forces systematically erode the

Portuguese army's control and by 1974 they had pushed as far south as Manica and Sofala, leaving the Portuguese army stretched and demoralized.

INDEPENDENCE

As the coup in Portugal 48 years earlier had changed the course of Mozambique's history, so did the one that took place in April 1974. The speed with which the new left-wing Portuguese government changed tack surprised all. Within five months they were meeting with FRELIMO leaders in Zambia's capital, Lusaka, to discuss arrangements for a cease-fire and the granting of independence. The cease-fire was implemented almost immediately and a provisional government consisting of six FRELIMO members and three representatives of Portugal was established to run the country during the period leading up to independence.

The initial reaction from the Portuguese settlers was one of anger and dismay. Many of them had only arrived during the last decade and all believed that they had been sold out. They sought to redress the situation, a small group actually managing to seize the main radio station and the international airport at then Lourenço Marques. There was an immediate response from the population who began to riot, as they believed their hard-fought struggle for freedom was in danger of being reversed. The combined government and FRELIMO forces managed to quell the uprisings, keeping the process on track, and Mozambique gained independence on 25 June 1975 with Samora Machel becoming the first president of the People's Republic of Mozambique. The Portuguese people expressed their sentiment about the new dispensation by fleeing to Portugal and South Africa in droves. In many cases they literally left everything, taking only what capital they could. At independence, roughly 50 per cent of all Portuguese had left Mozambique, that number rising to about 85 per cent by 1977.

After decades of being deprived of all political or economic power, the new government of Mozambique was totally under-prepared for rule as they set about reclaiming the country and its assets for the people. Samora Machel set the tone in his first speech as president when he aligned the country with the socialist nations of the world and promised to build on the ideals of the revolution. FRELIMO's first policy statement announced radical changes to the structure of the society and the economy, setting the country on the path of socialism. Among the changes announced were the nationalisation of all schools, private medical practices, mission clinics, radio stations and land, and all private legal practices were abolished. Home ownership was limited to one house per family.

Central to the new government's policies was the commitment to aid the liberation movements of neighbouring countries who, as yet, had not attained freedom. The most prominent of these were the African National Congress (ANC) in South Africa, and the Zimbabwe African National Union (ZANU) and Zimbabwe National People's Union (ZAPU) movements in then Rhodesia. This was implemented soon after independence, with Mozambique allowing the Rhodesian liberation forces to operate from Mozambique's central and northern provinces.

When the Rhodesian government decided to strike back, a series of cross-border raids and bloody skirmishes ensued. Issues became serious in 1976 when, within the space of a few months, Rhodesian forces attacked two villages and a refugee camp deep inside Mozambican territory and then sabotaged power and transport links in Tete Province. The FRELIMO administration, after consulting with other African leaders in the region, responded by closing the border with Rhodesia, at great economic cost to Mozambique, and offering increased assistance to the liberation forces.

In October 1977, the Mozambican army captured the first dissident who confirmed the existence of RENAMO or MNR (the Mozambique National Resistance Movement), and that the movement was being trained and equipped by the Rhodesian government. This

A haunting and sombre reminder of the civil war. This rusting tank lies alongside the main road in Sofala Province.

was the beginning of a prolonged and violent period in Mozambique's history involving a low-intensity war.

THE WAR YEARS

Many Mozambicans believe that the 15-year war between FRELIMO and RENAMO was the darkest and most traumatic period in their history, more so than the colonial era. Gaining independence had been a united struggle for the common good of all Mozambicans, whereas this conflict became a civil war that almost destroyed the soul of the country.

RENAMO came into being not because of a legitimate agenda, but rather to carry out policies of destruction and destabilization by the then governments of Rhodesia and subsequently South Africa. What began as a surrogate group of disaffected and mercenary soldiers, assembled and directed by the Rhodesian government, became a brutal and devastating force under the control of the South African apartheid regime.

The Rhodesians used RENAMO as an agent of sabotage against the Mozambican people and in joint-operation raids within the country, inflicting civilian losses and destroying vital transport and communication links. In 1980, Rhodesia became the independent state of Zimbabwe, leaving RENAMO without a cause and no funds with which to continue its existence. It was at this time that the South African government stepped forward to take control of the group with promises of increased funding, training and logistical support.

The South African leaders, at that stage, were gripped by the notion of a communist onslaught in Southern Africa and were of the opinion that the FRELIMO government was at the forefront of promoting the ideology. They were pursuing a policy of destabilization in certain neighbouring countries who opposed apartheid rule, believing that in so doing, they would create the climate within these countries for opponents of the ruling governments

to gain popularity and possibly take over on a basis more favourable to South Africa. An added reason to make use of RENAMO was to strike at ANC bases in Mozambique. RENAMO utilized this new alliance as an opportunity to improve their image and enhance their cause by officially announcing that they were a liberation movement fighting on behalf of the Mozambican people to remove the Marxist FRELIMO government.

History has now recorded that, in fact, Mozambique was no threat to the subcontinent and that RENAMO continued to act as a puppet organization, not involved in fighting a war of liberation, but rather carrying out ghastly atrocities against the people of Mozambique. So effective were they in doing this that by the mid-1980s RENAMO had grown in prominence, not because of support or legitimacy, but because by this stage the destruction they had wrought was taking its toll on the country and its people.

The countryside has been almost completely cleared of landmines. This minefield is being de-activated by the Halo Trust.

In March 1984 the governments of Mozambique and South Africa took the first steps towards peace by signing the Nkomati Accord, a pact of 'non-aggression and good neighbourliness'. This was followed in October 1984 by the Pretoria Declaration: an agreement which should have been signed between the government and RENAMO but it became a dead letter. Neither of these accords were really successful as the attacks by RENAMO continued and South Africa was constantly accused by Mozambique of continuing its financial support for the rebel group.

In October 1986, President Samora Machel was killed under suspicious circumstances when his aircraft, returning from a meeting of Southern African leaders in Zambia, crashed on South African soil. His successor, Joaquim Chissano, took a more pragmatic approach to both the issue of RENAMO and the existing Socialist system. He realized that the rebels would have to be included in any solution that hoped to end the country's slide into extreme chaos and accepted the need to move towards a market economy.

By this stage the dual impacts had reduced the country to a state of collapse and had ruined the infrastructure, particularly in the rural areas. RENAMO's claims of being a liberation movement for the people were negated by its strategy of specifically attacking rural villages and spreading fear among the populace. In many instances they concentrated their assaults on health and educational facilities, often killing the trained staff running these clinics and schools. They also burnt crops, contaminated water supplies, looted factories, blew up power lines and mined vast areas of the countryside and the transport routes, all contributing to making the rural areas hazardous for

Football is the most popular sport in Mozambique with weekend matches taking place all over the country.

The national flag of Mozambique. The country gained independence in 1975.

the government and the aid agencies attempting to bring relief to the impoverished people.

As in most wars, the people who suffered most were the innocent citizens trying to eke out an existence under harrowing circumstances. This was starkly brought home to the world when, after the peace accords were signed in October 1992, some 1,4 million external refugees needed to be repatriated and close on two million people had been displaced inside their own country. It is generally accepted that, outside of being involved in the laying of land mines and isolated cases of violence and

looting, the FRELIMO forces did not display anywhere near the same destructive appetite as their foes. Under-staffed and underequipped, the army struggled to maintain their defenses in the rural areas and along strategic lines, allowing RENAMO free reign in many parts of the country.

It was not until 1990 that the impasse began to break. The FRELIMO government drafted a new constitution introducing major political reform based on a multiparty regime and direct elections for the presidency and the 250-member People's Assembly. The draft contained sufficient changes to encourage RENAMO to begin discussing the possibility of a permanent cease-fire and working towards national reconciliation.

MOZAMBIQUE TODAY

THE PEACE ACCORD AND MULTI-PARTY ELECTIONS

The first meeting between the government and RENAMO took place in Rome in July 1990, followed by three further rounds of talks which culminated in the first joint initiative, a Joint Verification

Commission to monitor a partial cease-fire. A series of negotiations followed, aimed at eliminating differences hindering the parties from signing a permanent peace agreement. In October 1991, both parties forged a major breakthrough with the signing of a protocol that contained a set of principles to guide future negotiations for a permanent peace accord. The General Peace Agreement was finally signed in Rome on 4 October 1992 by President Joaquim Chissano and RENAMO leader Afonso Dhlakama, and came into force on 15 October 1992.

Under the terms of the agreement, the most crucial matter was the immediate general cease-fire and the withdrawal of troops from both sides to designated assembly points. Under United Nations supervision (a force of 7,500 troops, supervisors and police officials known as the UN Operation in Mozambique [ONUMOZ] arrived in early 1993), both armies were to be demobilized and a unified defence force with equal numbers from both sides to be created. This process, after lengthy delays caused by confusion over the assembly points and the general reluctance of soldiers to report there, was eventually completed in August 1994 with the inauguration of the Forças Armadas de Defesa de Moçambique (FADM).

The other major point in the agreement was that UN-supervised elections were to be held within one year of the successful implementation of the General Peace Agreement. Again, RENAMO engaged in obstructive politics by setting new conditions and demands during the period leading up to the elections.

The elections were finally held over three days of voting on 27–29 October 1994. A third day of voting had to be added, because RENAMO chose to boycott the elections the day before voting began, claiming that conditions for a free and fair result were not in place. With UN patience wearing thin at RENAMO's disruptive tactics, the election went

This roadside tailor has set up his informal business at the Save River bridge toll stop.

ahead while international pressure was brought to bear on Afonso Dhlakama's participation. He conceded and re-entered the election on the second day of voting.

Joaquim Chissano won the presidency with an outright majority of 53.3 per cent. Dhlakama gained 33.7 per cent of the votes with the remaining votes going to ten rival candidates. In the legislative election FRELIMO gained 44.3 per cent of the votes, giving the party 129 seats in the Assembly, RENAMO 37.7 per cent of the votes and 112 seats, the coalition party, the Democratic Union (UD), gained 5.1 per cent of the votes and the remaining 9 seats. Numerous smaller parties collected the remaining percentage, none gaining sufficient support to win any seats in the assembly.

An interesting observation arising from the country's first free election was that after nineteen years of single-party rule, the race was contested by 25 parties and there was a 90 per cent voter turnout, an overwhelming endorsement

of the new course the country was following. Joaquim Chissano was inaugurated as President on 9 December 1994. The new government was formed on 16 December and sworn in on 23 December 1994.

GOVERNMENT

The Republic of Mozambique's constitution was drawn up and ratified in November 1990, replacing fifteen years of single-party rule, and was slightly amended in 1996. It enshrines the following main principles:

* The country is an independent and sovereign state, promoting freedom, democracy, human rights and social justice.
* A Bill of Rights respects and protects all citizens before the law, irrespective of race, sex, religion, class or ethnic origin. There is no death penalty.
* Individual rights are guaranteed, including freedom of press, speech and association.
* Political participation is guaranteed to all citizens over 18 years of age and is exercised through universal and secret suffrage. The promotion or use of violence by political parties is prohibited.
* The state is entitled to call on all citizens to defend the country.

The political system is a multiparty democracy with the electorate going to the polls every five years. Governing the country are a legislative and executive arm, both running concurrently for the five-year period. The legislature is a unicameral system with the 250 elected members operating from a single chamber, known as the Assembly of the Republic. Members, known as deputies, sit for two periods a year, but may be called into session by the president at any other time. The executive function is performed by the Council of Ministers, which consists of 19 portfolios, a Secretary General and a Prime Minister, all appointed by the President who is the head of state, government and the armed forces. The Prime Minister assists the President with the duties of government and acts as the leading spokesperson on policies in the Assembly. Local government is carried out by appointed governors in each of the eleven provinces who administer a total of 139 municipalities and 394 administrative posts.

The judiciary is independent, and comprises the Supreme Court and various regional courts as well as courts dealing with customs, labour, business and maritime issues. They are entrusted by the Constitution to uphold the principles of the Constitution, and to defend the rights of the country's citizens. The President appoints the Attorney General and the professional judges of the Supreme Court. The Administrative Court is responsible for the supervision of public expenditure and efficient administration by public officials.

Mozambique is a full member of the United Nations, the Organization of African Unity, the Commonwealth, the Southern African Development Community, the World Bank and the International Monetary Fund (IMF).

THE ECONOMY

The economy of Mozambique is typical of a developing country. It is based on primary product activity, and in economic parlance, is grouped as a Least Developed Country. For the years 1988–1990 the World Bank listed Mozambique as the world's poorest country in terms of per capita income, and over the period 1988–1992 it was one of the world's biggest recipients of donor aid as a percentage of gross domestic product (GDP). Having endured years of low, and at times negative, growth during the war, the country experienced a turnaround in its fortunes during the early 1990s, the upturn coinciding with the peace process. Although it now sustains annual growth rates of 5 per cent plus, the economy and country still labours under the strains of the damage caused in the past, and needs more time and investment to overcome poverty and under-development.

The first and probably the most fundamental reason for Mozambique's situation, as with most former African colonies, was the exploitative conduct of its colonizers, whose commitment to judicious and beneficial development for all peoples of the country was limited in the extreme. The final act of Mozambique's colonizers was to flee the country in droves at independence, stripping it of much of its capital and skilled labour. The effect was calamitous, creating a vacuum with which the new government was ill-equipped to deal.

The second reason was that fifteen years of civil conflict almost completely wiped out the country's infrastructure and social services as well as stunting all forms of progress during that period, with the war absorbing the scant foreign reserves being generated at the time. Power stations, road and rail links, rural schools, hospitals, clinics and factories were, in most cases, laid to waste. During the war, both sides made extensive use of land mines to the extent that immediately after the war, many zones became no-go areas. Although the country is now almost completely de-mined, the funds and efforts required to achieve this held back development and the rebuilding of the infrastructure.

Lastly, the FRELIMO government that took power in 1975 embarked on socialist policies, a system that centralized the control of production and pricing, and left the allocation of resources in the hands of the state, at the expense of the private sector. The system broke down due to the war and management failures, and the economy collapsed.

These factors all contributed to an alarming economic decline, with the World Bank's statistics showing that from 1980–1988 the country's GDP rate sank to a negative 3,5 per cent per annum average. Commodity exports fell 72 per cent, inflation reached triple digit figures and government debt rose substantially as expenditure soared and revenues declined, creating a mess that the government recognised had to change.

In 1984, in an attempt to reverse the decline, the government began to amend its policies, and by embarking on a freer market-based system. The changes showed modest yet crucial improvements, encouraging FRELIMO to introduce a full Economic Recovery Programme of structural adjustment in 1987, with the support of the World Bank, IMF and international donor agencies. Tangible improvements only started showing once the war had

This modern BP service station is situated in Nampula, the capital of Nampula Province.

Other than in Maputo Province, bananas grow well throughout the country.

ended, when local and international investors and donors began injecting capital into long-term projects.

Today, impressive monetary and growth figures are being achieved, and exports are increasing annually, earning valuable foreign exchange with which goods and services can now be bought. Inflation has been reduced from over 63 per cent in 1994 to below 10 per cent currently. The economy achieved a seven per cent growth rate in 1997 and is forecast to improve on that figure over the next two years. Income per capita has increased from $80 in 1989 to $126 in 1997. Most importantly, foreign investment is returning to the country with capital being committed to a variety of ventures, the most talked about being the Maputo Corridor project, which is expected to involve upwards of 15 billion rands.

The Cahora Bassa hydroelectric power project has been revived and will eventually cater for all of Mozambique's electricity requirements. Various South African mining houses are involved in developing facilities for processing raw materials such as coal, gas, iron ore and aluminium. Brewing plants in the capital city are being refurbished and upgraded by the world's fourth largest brewery, South African Breweries.

Oil exploration has begun in earnest, with BP Mozambique involved in off-shore drilling in an 80,000 square kilometre (30,890 square miles) concession between Beira and Quelimane. The most significant sign of a change in economic direction is the decision to open the Maputo Stock Exchange.

The various aid and development agencies involved within Mozambique must be given credit for helping to keep the economy alive during the country's worst periods. Their contribution towards the local economies has been substantial in both monetary and educational terms.

Most of these agencies are international, receiving funds from the United States of America, the United Kingdom, Scandinavia, Australia, France and Germany, among others. Their work has entailed operating at local levels, in conjunction with government, to initiate and promote socio-economic activity aimed at improving the lives of the communities, in spheres ranging from agricultural, road rehabilitation, health and education to water projects. While they have played a hugely constructive part, any long-term reliance on their role in the economy would be a regressive direction for the economic planners to take.

MINING AND GAS

Other than tantalite, Mozambique does not possess any mineral deposits of significant quality. Although the ore bodies that are presently known to exist have to date been under-exploited, geological surveys show sufficient reserves for commercial exploitation well into the future. The tantalite deposits at Murroa in Zambezia are some of the world's largest and the coal reserves at Moatize near Tete are estimated at 1,000 million tons. A large iron ore deposit has been discovered at Namapa in northern Nampula but is yet to be exploited, as are the smaller deposits around Tete.

The gold deposits in Manica Province have not been thoroughly assessed, but are thought to be viable for mining on a medium scale. Bauxite is mined in small quantities in the provinces of Tete and Manica, and copper at

Planting rice on the fertile floodplains of the Limpopo River.

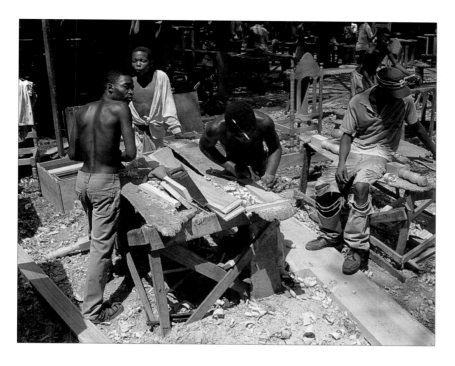

Carpenters at work in the outdoor furniture market in Xai-Xai. The town lies 10 kilometres (6 miles) inland from the coast and is well equipped to serve holiday-makers.

Mundonguara, also in Manica. Deposits of asbestos, diamonds, manganese, uranium, titanium and semi-precious stones do exist but have yet to be capitalized. Extensive natural gas fields occur in the Pande and Temande regions, due to be brought into full production before the year 2000, with a 900-kilometre-long (560-mile) gas pipeline between Pande and South Africa under construction.

AGRICULTURE, FORESTRY AND FISHING

Agriculture is the foundation of the Mozambican economy. In the past, it contributed upwards of 65 per cent to gross domestic product in favourable years, while in recent years the sector's contribution has fallen as the economy has diversified, with the 1995 figure below 40 per cent. At least 75 per cent of the economically active population are in some way involved in this sector, the majority practising some form of subsistence agriculture.

Agriculture also has the most potential for major increases in capacity and efficiency, highlighted by the fact that less than 10 per cent of arable land is cultivated. Presently, the system is in the process of changing from one of state ownership to privately run estates and co-operatives. The first steps were taken in the early 1990s when state enterprises were sold off to groups of local farmers, and has gained momentum with the involvement of foreign companies in restoring many of the sugar estates, and cotton and cashew nut plantations.

The most fertile and productive regions are the northern provinces of Cabo Delgado, Niassa and Nampula, the coastal plains of Zambezia and Sofala, and the central regions of Manica, with the major industrial companies of Madal, Entreposto, Lomaco and João Ferreira dos Santos (J.F.S) all having extensive agricultural interests throughout. The southern provinces suffer from poor soils. The country's most important export

crops are cashew nuts, coconut (copra), tea, cotton and sugar, and the main internal market crops include maize, bananas, cassava, citrus and rice, with maize and cassava being the primary subsistence crops. Floods, droughts and cyclones all have an impact on the annual success of the agricultural industry, and because of the presence of tsetse fly in the north, the cattle ranching industry is established south of the Save River, its stronghold in Maputo Province.

The central provinces of Sofala, Manica and Zambezia have traditionally been timber producing regions but with the expansion of the industry, the northern provinces of Cabo Delgado and Nampula have been opened up to concessionaires. The port of Pemba is now the leading point of export for the industry. Logging and the processing of raw timber into sawn boards are the dominant commercial activities, with over 90 per cent of product being exported to South Africa, Zimbabwe and the East. The country has over one million hectares (two and half million acres) of commercially productive woodland consisting mainly of Umbila (*Pterocarpus angolensis*), Pau-Ferro (*Swartzia madagascariensis*), Jambire or Panga-Panga (*Milletia stuhlmannii*), and Chanfuta (*Afzelia quanzensis*) trees. Plantations of pine and eucalyptus are exploited in the provinces of Manica and Sofala. The need for wood fuel accounts for a fair proportion of the annual timber consumption in the form of charcoal, produced by a process of slow combustion in closed pits dug into the earth.

Although having Africa's longest coastline along the Indian Ocean, the country does not have a well-developed fishing industry. Shellfish and prawns form the largest contribution to this sector. The sustainable pelagic fishing reserves per annum are estimated at 500,000 tons, although presently only 25 per cent of this level is being achieved. To improve on catches the government has entered into joint ventures with Japan, Spain, Portugal, Russia and South Africa.

A fishing crew heads for home after a long day at sea on the azure waters of Fernão Veloso.

A large number of the coastal-dwelling population is involved in subsistence fishing, making use of a variety of techniques, from the more traditional methods of spearing, hand-lining and the setting of fish traps to using gill and seine nets hauled from dhows and motorized vessels. The sector has been given a boost with the advent of the kapenta industry on Cahora Bassa Dam, which is able to produce an estimated 8,000 tons of fish per annum.

MANUFACTURING

The mass exodus of skilled labour and capital after independence had the most adverse effect on the manufacturing sector with many factories and production plants being abandoned or sabotaged. The government's answer was to intervene in most of these units and turn them over to worker's committees. Advisers and technicians brought in from many countries, including the Soviet Bloc, had mixed success.

What remained of the manufacturing sector was again hit during the war, and still today, the outskirts of Maputo bear testimony to the destruction of its factories and industrial plants. Relief was only introduced with the economic reform programmes announced in the 1980s. The situation has fortunately improved in the last decade as the government, along with the help of donor aid and foreign investors, has undertaken a major rehabilitation programme.

Manufacturing is confined predominantly to the processing of primary products, such as hardwoods and agricultural products, with the Maputo area producing over 50 per cent of total output. Beira, Nampula, Quelimane and Chimoio are important secondary areas, all due to benefit in the growth expected to materialize from the Beira and Nacala corridor projects. The principal industry is food-processing, with sugar, maize and cashews the most important products. Secondary industries include chemicals, beverages, textiles, cement and glass, while products such as sisal, tea, timber and cotton are processed for export. Light engineering is still a relatively small component of this sector.

TOURISM

The hopes and expectations of the country are highlighted by the Directorate of National Tourism's publicity campaign whose slogan is 'The New Mozambique – Rhythm of Change'. Tourism has enormous potential and this industry can be turned into a thriving foreign exchange earner. Equally significant is the crucial role that tourism will play in improving the country's tarnished image.

Many remember the pre-war days of sun-filled vacations in the tropics, and balmy weekends in what was then known as Lourenço Marques. Records show that, in 1973, over 200,000 visitors, mostly from South Africa, then Rhodesia and Portugal, toured Mozambique. However, for close on twenty years after independence the country experienced a total dearth of tourists. The combined effects of regional politics and the ravages of war not only dissuaded potential visitors but also saw the existing facilities degenerate through destruction and neglect. At the time of independence in 1975, Mozambique had accommodation capacity of over 8,000 beds, that number falling to a mere 1,000 by 1989.

It was in the early 1990s, coinciding with the government's change of heart and the end of the war, that tourists began returning in modest numbers. Over the last few years the influx has grown dramatically, and the industry is set to again achieve its full potential. New hotels, lodges and related

expenditure have contributed roughly 10 per cent to total fixed investment over this same period and according to the Directorate of National Tourism, almost a hundred new projects have been approved.

The Government and the Directorate of National Tourism have shown their commitment to the industry by drawing up a national policy on tourism known as the Strategy for the Development of Tourism in Mozambique. The policy has firm objectives and principles and provides guidelines for the way forward. The core of the plan is the demarcation of the country into 19 separate Partial Protection Zones based on their ability to attract visitors, their accessibility and their capacity to cater for the expected levels of development. The expectations are not only for the industry to attract foreign investment and become a major source of foreign revenue, but also to offer employment opportunties and empowerment to local economies.

Mozambique is most definitely in the process of being rediscovered as an exciting outdoor destination on the African subcontinent. Its obvious delights are strung out along the country's vast

and varied coastline, offering the visitor everything imaginable in the way of water sports. For those prepared to tackle the hinterland and its, at times, testing infrastructure and amenities, there is plenty to do and see that is impressive and worthwhile. The country has much to experience in the way of wildlife and natural history with the vast inland areas and their rich diversity of ecosystems providing exciting destinations for birders, hikers, mountaineers and naturalists.

An interesting historical and cultural heritage awaits discovery, promising a charming alternative to the traditional beach holiday. Apart from the Bazaruto Archipelago hosting two or three visits a month from scheduled cruise liners, Mozambique is not yet geared for mass tourism. No one area is blessed with a full range of activities and access can, at times, be restricted, but the situation is ideal for special interest tourism and adventure seekers.

A note of caution is needed with regard to the sensitivity of many of the wilderness areas and their ability to sustain the increasing numbers of people who are visiting them. Without the necessary laws and regulations to protect the fauna and flora, as well as the manpower to police them, the country's resources may well suffer from excessive and uncontrolled usage. Sections of the coastline are being invaded by a multitude of divers, fishermen and four-wheel-drive enthusiasts, often without due concern for the environment or the people whose land it is.

If measures are not introduced in the near future to curb thoughtless and reckless behaviour, many of these sites will be damaged or even destroyed for future generations. The wildlife populations are scant, yet hunting continues to feature as a major attraction to foreigners without the necessary research having been done to validate the quotas. Tourism should be a non-consumptive renewable 'natural resource', and if managed correctly, can be of far greater long-term value than the traditional industrial and agricultural economic sectors.

The coastal town of Ponta do Ouro, very popular with scuba divers.

SOUTHERN MOZAMBIQUE

Opposite: *Introduced by the Arabs, the dhow is synonymous with the coastal-dwelling communities of Mozambique.*
Above*: Goats range the dunes on Bazaruto Island in search of greenery.*

The southern regions of Mozambique are made up of Maputo, Gaza and Inhambane provinces, with the country's capital, Maputo, lying in the extreme south, less than 100 kilometres (62 miles) from both the borders of South Africa and Swaziland.

The capital also shares its name with the geographical area of Maputaland which stretches from Maputo Bay south to South Africa's Lake St Lucia. It includes the Maputo Elephant Reserve and the ancient migratory trails of the area's remaining elephant populations.

At the northern extreme of the region lies Mozambique's most popular tourist destination, the Bazaruto Archipelago. This group of islands ranks in impact and in scenic beauty with other African attractions such as the Okavango Delta, Victoria Falls, Lake Kariba and the Serengeti Plains, and offers so much more in terms of activities than the better known destinations of Mauritius, the Comores and Zanzibar. Added to this is the solitude experienced at the islands' resorts, whose beaches are without the madding crowds found elsewhere in the Indian Ocean.

The stretch of coastline between Xai-Xai and Inhassoro follows closely as a prime holiday destination, and visitors flock to its resort towns for good reason: the many beautiful beaches fringed by vast coconut palm groves, the numerous bays and river mouths, and the safe, crystal-clear waters combine to create the holiday of a lifetime.

Above: *Albino, the doorman at the Polana Hotel.*
Top right: *Clube Naval, a privately owned yachting and recreational centre in Maputo, is a favourite with the Portuguese community.*
Opposite top: *The southern side of Maputo is known as Catembe, linked to the capital by a ferry which makes hourly crossings throughout the day.*
Right: *The 200-roomed Polana Hotel, overlooking the waters of Maputo Bay, was built in 1922. Extensive renovations were carried out in 1990, upgrading one of Maputo's finest hotels to international standards.*

Opposite: *The stately, neoclassical city hall, built in 1945, fronts onto the Praça de Independência.*
Left: *Children peer out from the ruins of a Maputo home.*
Below: *Known as Lourenço Marques during colonial times, the capital changed its name to Maputo at independence in 1975.*
Bottom: *The Natural History Museum is known for its display of elephant foetuses, covering the animal's full 22-month gestation period. The building's architectural style is referred to as Manueline.*

Above: *A wall mural at the Praça dos Herois (Heroes Square) commemorates the country's revolutionary victory over Portuguese colonialism. The mural prominently depicts the late Samora Machel, Mozambique's first president at independence, and honours the role played by soldiers and the working class.*

Right: *Silverio Sitoe is one of Mozambique's best known artists. He is one of the select few who get to exhibit their work in Europe, particularly in Portugal.*

Above: *Cashew nuts have long been a sought-after purchase by visitors to Maputo's lively markets.*
Right: *The city's fish markets are always well stocked with an assortment of fresh fish, prawns, crab and calamari.*

Left: *The fruit and vegetable stalls situated in the Mercado Municipal on Av. 25 de Setembro offer fresh supplies on a daily basis.*
Below: *Much of Maputo's local economy still takes place in informal markets. Here a liquor vendor takes an afternoon nap.*

Above: *Water hyacinth, an exotic plant introduced from South America, is becoming a problem on all rivers south of the Zambezi. These alien plants block up the river systems and do not have a natural predator to control their growth.*

Right: *Two Shangaan youths with reeds cut from the Limpopo flood-plains. The reeds will be used as building materials.*

Opposite top: *Julio Maelo, right, shows a worker how to cut bananas on the SOCA co-operative in Gaza Province.*

Opposite bottom: *Fishermen net for prawns along the muddy banks of the Limpopo River.*

Opposite, Above and Left: *The majority of Mozambique's rural citizens belong to one of a variety of churches which mix Judaeo-Christian teachings with traditional beliefs. Here, the pastor of a Church of Zion congregation near Xai-Xai performs a baptism ceremony.*
Pages 58-59: *Dhows, used as the main form of transport to link the many coastal fishing communities, are made from solid wood and propelled by a large canvas main sail.*

57

Top and Above: *Clothing markets in the Inhambane district.*
Left: *Mozambique's abundant tropical fruits can be bought cheaply in most village markets.*
Opposite: *A waiter from Barra Lodge holds up a poster put out by the Inhambane Tourism Association.*

Above: *Morrungulo Lodge nestles below an extensive canopy of palm trees. Most of the beach resorts in the southern region offer a variety of accommodation options, from camping to self-catering chalets.*

Opposite top: *Sunseekers relaxing in the warm waters of a rock pool at Pomene.*
Opposite bottom: *The beach at Pomene features a prominent outcrop of fossilized coral rock.*

Left: *From Vilanculos, the white sands of Magaruque Island shimmer in the distance, approximately 15 kilometres (9,5 miles) away.*

Page 66 Top: *Net fishing is widely practised along the coast. A preferred method is to leave one end of the net on the shoreline while the other is carried out in a wide arc by a rowing boat.*

Page 66 Bottom: *A late-night trader displays his goods by the light of a paraffin lamp.*

Page 67: *The view of the Hotel Dona Ana looking across the small fishing harbour at Vilanculos.*

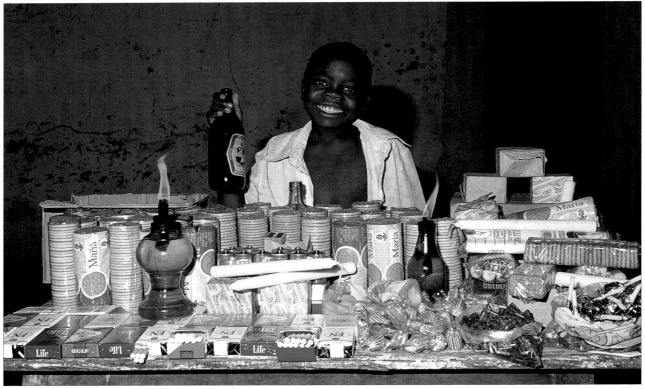

Opposite top: *Supplying the lodges on the Bazaruto Archipelago with provisions is done mostly by dhow.*
Opposite bottom: *The lighthouse on Bazaruto Island.*
Below: *A view of Bazaruto Island's dunes and lagoons.*

Pages 70-71: *Fishing is a way of life for the residents of the Bazaruto Archipelago. The menfolk from the villages get together at least once a day, most often at the change of tides, to work the large nets.*

Above: *Having helped pack the fishing nets away, this boy takes a breather.*
Right: *A colourful paint job.*
Opposite top: *After the day's catch, a group of children take in the gentle evening sun.*
Opposite bottom: *Throw-netting is a technique used for fishing on the changing tides.*

Left: *A spectacular coral shelf in the Indian Ocean. The warm Mozambique current and clear waters attract diving enthusiasts to the magnificent coastline.*
Below and Opposite: *Hermit crabs and coral trout form part of the colourful marine life that abounds on Mozambique's many offshore coral reefs.*

Above and Right: *Indigo Bay Lodge and Bazaruto Lodge are well positioned on the southern and northern ends respectively of Bazaruto Island.*
Opposite top left: *Large numbers of pansy shells can be collected while walking the tidal zone of Pansy Island, a short distance from Benguerra Lodge.*
Opposite top right: *Ghost crabs (Ocypode ceratophthalmus) are found along the beaches on the Archipelago's islands.*
Opposite bottom: *An island sunset.*

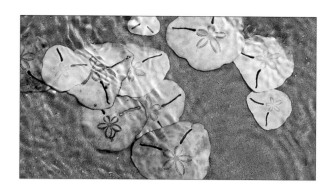

Pages 78-79: *Fishing dhows lie at anchor against the backdrop of a Bazaruto sunset. Vistas like these are an appealing feature of the islands.*
Right: *Bathtime for a young island child.*
Below: *Children strolling along the beach at low tide on Benguerra Island.*

Top: *The islands have become popular fly-fishing destinations. This king mackerel was taken on a sinking line off Benguerra Island.*
Left: *The catch of the day. What is not needed for the table is released back into the sea by the boat skippers.*
Above: *Charter yachts at anchor off Benguerra Lodge.*

81

Right: *A guest at Benguerra Lodge relaxes, island-style.*
Pages 84-85: *The double-sailed dhows of the region are mostly used for deep-sea commercial fishing trips.*

CENTRAL REGION

Opposite: *A saddle-billed stork cuts a solitary pose in the fading sunset.*
Above: *The hot springs at the foot of Mount Morrumbala, one of numerous such sites in the central regions.*

Mozambique's central regions, made up of the provinces of Sofala, Manica, Tete and Zambezia, cover the largest part of the country and thus offer the traveller diversity in terms of both geographic features and destination appeal. The land includes the highlands of Manica which run along the border with Zimbabwe and then descend through the flatter central regions of Sofala and Zambezia to the low-lying swamplands of the coastal stretches.

Some of the region's main attractions are the shores of the Chicamba Real Dam, Gorongosa National Park and its surrounding mountains and forests, Cahora Bassa Dam and the Zambezi Valley. Tete is the dry, hot area of the country, at times very dry and very hot: it is not unknown for the daytime temperatures along the Zambezi Valley to consistently measure in the mid-40s (around 115 °F) during the months of November through to January.

An idea of the change in climate type is visible on the journey north from Manica to Tete Province, as miombo woodland gives way to the harsher landscapes of acacia and mopane woodland. Tete is also baobab tree country, often found in forest clusters throughout the central and northern regions.

Below: *Prior to independence, Beira enjoyed a reputation of entertaining holiday-makers in splendid style. During this period, the now run-down Grand Hotel was a popular destination for those seeking out the finest.*
Right: *The Judicial Court for Sofala Province is situated in Beira.*

88

Above: *The Púngoè River flows across the central regions of Sofala Province before reaching its mouth south of Beira.*
Right: *The ruins of war. Gorongosa National Park is thankfully on its way to full rehabilitation.*

Above: *Keen bird-watchers will know the upper slopes of Mount Gorongosa as the home of the greenheaded oriole.*
Left: *Fishing in the fast-flowing waters of the Vunduzi River.*

Pages 92-93: *The* marimba *is a popular instrument throughout the central regions. The combination of kiaat crossplanks and empty pumpkin pods create the instrument's resonant sound.*
Above: *Clay pots are still made and used in the rural areas of the central and northern regions.*
Right and Opposite: *Maize is first strained through a sieve and sorted before it is ready for pounding.*

Opposite and Above: *On the outskirts of Manica, a gold rush is still on in the foothills of the surrounding mountains.*

Left: *The many Roman Catholic cathedrals found throughout Mozambique are a legacy of Portuguese colonial rule. This one stands atop the hills surrounding the town of Manica.* **Above:** *The entrance to a local restaurant in Manica.*

Below: *This monument outside Vila de Sena honours past colonial governors.*
Bottom: *A shop's welcoming sign.*
Right: *The main façade of the Jesuit Mission of Boroma. The mission was built in 1890 on the banks of the Zambezi River a short distance from Tete town.*

Pages 102-103: *Heading home, this lone fisherman paddles through the remains of trees claimed by the rising waters of Cahora Bassa Dam.*
Left and Bottom: *Two of the more common species found throughout Mozambique are the fish eagle and the little egret.*

Left, Below and Bottom: *Mozambique is a bird-watcher's paradise. The high species count is primarily due to the wide variety of habitats. Seen here are a greyhooded kingfisher (left), an immature Cape gannet (below) and a goliath heron (bottom).*

Left: *Kapenta rigs on Cahora Bassa Dam head out at sunset for the night's catch. The small pelagic fish were introduced into the dam from Lake Kariba in Zimbabwe.*
Above: *Kapenta are sun-dried for up to eight hours on drying racks.*
Pages 108-109: *Early morning on the Shire River.*

Above: *The Quelimane clothing market. Markets in Mozambique also function as an important meeting place for the community.*
Right: *Looking down Av. Samora Machel in Quelimane. This is the view from the dining room of the Hotel Chuabo.*

Left: *Temporary housing is constructed from various parts of the coconut tree.*
Below: *This herd of water buffalo among the coconut plantations of Grupo Madal is reputed to be the only herd in Mozambique.*
Bottom: *These salt processing pits are located on the outskirts of Quelimane.*

Pages 112-113: *Grupo Madal is the largest producer of copra in Mozambique. Here the collected coconuts await processing.*
Opposite: *Manual labour is used to retrieve the hard-to-reach coconuts.*
Above left: *The fruit's husk is removed and the shell split in half before the drying begins.*
Above right: *Ripe Malaysian coconuts.*
Right: *A close-up of the various processing stages, from the unopened coconuts to the dried fruit.*

NORTHERN MOZAMBIQUE

Opposite: *A pensive young Makua girl.*
Above: *Most of the cloth sold in Mozambique's markets is imported from the East. Shades of orange, red and yellow are the choice colours in the north.*

The country's northern regions are the least well known and less travelled parts of Mozambique, but the provinces of Nampula, Niassa and Cabo Delgado offer some of the most dramatic and beautiful destinations in the country.

What the area lacks in terms of infrastructure and facilities is more than compensated for by its immense scenic beauty and its fascinating cultural and historical aspects.

Although Nampula City is the third largest in Mozambique and Ilha de Moçambique a culturally and historically rich island, both lie over 2,300 kilometres (1,430 miles) by road away from Maputo, probably the main reason why they have remained relatively undiscovered.

It is worth noting that travellers wishing to gain maximum enjoyment out of a trip to Mozambique's more remote regions north of Pemba should make use of a reliable four-wheel-drive vehicle, and only after having researched local weather and road conditions. Sufficient supplies of fresh food, water and fuel need to be taken along, as availability of these commodities is unreliable.

Above: *Massive inselberg formations provide an imposing backdrop to the main road linking Nampula and Cuamba.*
Left: *Late afternoon sunlight casts an air of tranquillity over the Cuamba countryside.*
Opposite: *Bicycles are the main form of private transport in the country's rural areas. Here reed mats and roosters are loaded for the trip home.*

Opposite and Above: *Rice, a major subsistence crop in the northern provinces, is harvested during the winter months.*
Left: *The provinces of Niassa and Nampula are the major cotton producing areas of Mozambique.*
Page 122: *The Catholic cathedral on Ilha de Moçambique was built in 1556, destroyed by the Dutch in the early 1600s, and rebuilt in 1635 by the Portuguese.*
Page 123: *The Palácio de São Paulo was built as a Jesuit college before being used as a residence by Portuguese governors. Now restored, it serves as a museum housing fine examples of Portuguese art and furniture.*

Pages 124-125: *The central mosque in the Arab quarter overlooks the narrow stretch of water separating Ilha de Moçambique from the mainland.*
Left and Above: *The Sanctuary of Mary Mother of God in the Namialo district was built as a Catholic mission station in 1941 before becoming a parish in 1988.*
Opposite top: *The derelict parish of São Antonio on Ilha de Moçambique.*
Opposite bottom left and right: *Intricate masonry on buildings from the northern regions.*

Right: *Makua children play among fishing nets on Ilha de Moçambique.*
Opposite top and bottom: *Fishing is the principal source of income for the inhabitants of Ilha de Moçambique. Fish that is not consumed on the island is sent to the markets in Nampula.*

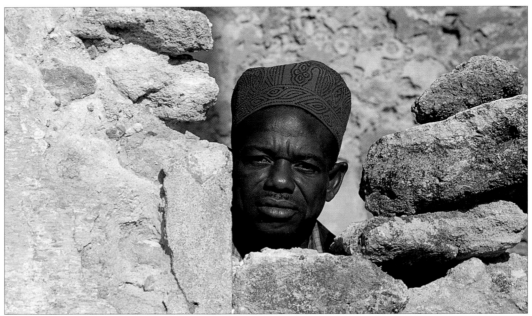

Opposite top left and right: *Inside Fortaleza de São Sebastião on Ilha de Moçambique. Construction on this impressive fort began in 1554 and was only completed in the early 1600s.*
Opposite bottom: *The majority of the island's inhabitants are Muslim.*
Left: *The fort fronts onto the sea on three sides. The Dutch invaded Ilha de Moçambique three times during the late 1500s and early 1600s, but never succeeded in capturing the stronghold.*
Above: *Cannons on the Fortaleza de São Sebastião's ramparts.*

Pages 132-133: *A Pemba fishing village.*
ABOVE: *Makua women adorn their faces with a paste made from a mixture of root extract and water.*
Right: *A Makua dance group performs for the local villagers on Ilha de Moçambique. Many of the dances embrace Arabic influences.*
Opposite: *Portrait of a Makua woman from Angoche.*

Left: *The Complexo Turístico Nautilus in Pemba is the premier destination for visitors to the north. This is the view from the resort's beach bar.*
Pages 138-139: *An idyllic beach setting: the palm-lined beach and sapphire waters of Wimbe Beach in Pemba.*

Opposite: *One of numerous mangrove channels linking the islands of Ibo and Quirimbas.*
Above: *Mangroves are the only tree species that have adapted to survival in salty tidal zones.*
Left: *The aerial roots, or pneumatophores, of the red mangrove (*Rhizophora mucronata*).*

Left: *The entrance to Fort Alezi. The fort was built in 1791 on the island of Ibo.*
Below: *The painted face of a young Makua woman.*
Opposite: *Inside Fort Alezi, the island's silversmiths painstakingly carry on their traditional craft of making trinkets and jewellery from old coins and pieces of antique silver.*

Above: *Makua women drive fish towards their nets on the tidal flats of Quirimbas Island.*
Left: *A joyful celebration takes place after a successful haul.*

Left: *Fishing dhows moored on the northwestern tip of Quirimbas Island.*
Below: *The far northern coastal town of Palma is set among expansive coconut groves.*

Right: *Facial tattoos were a form of adornment practised by earlier generations but are now only seen on some of the older folk.*
Below: *The district of Palma is well-known for its skilled mat weavers, such as these women seen displaying their colourful wares.*
Opposite: *This Makua woman's natural beauty is enhanced by her accessories. The headwrap is a legacy of the Arabic and the nose ring of the Indian influence.*

Opposite: *Collecting water is a social event traditionally carried out by the womenfolk of the family. The government, with the help of donor agencies, has laid on waterpoints in most rural towns and villages.*

Above and Left: *Colourful headwraps are a clothing feature worn by the women in the northern regions.*

Left: *A village scene in the Palma district.*
Below: *Colourful mats for everyday use are made from woven palm fronds and dyed with a combination of root extracts and modern synthetic colourings.*
Opposite: *The rough gravel main road north from Mocímboa da Praia to Palma at times becomes impassable during the summer rains.*

Opposite: *A masked Makonde dancer from the Mueda district. The name 'Mapico' is used for both the mask and the dance performed.*

Above: *An elderly Makonde woman showing facial tattoos and an upper lip plug (known as an 'ndona'), both of which are forms of adornment.*

Opposite: *An aerial view of the bold inselberg scenery found in the Niassa Reserve.*
Above: *The Niassa Reserve carries the highest numbers of game in Mozambique, including elephant, seen here.*
Left: *Mark Jenkins, left, is the operations manager for the reserve.*
Pages 156-157: *The Lugenda River forms the southern and western boundary of the Niassa Reserve before flowing into the Rovuma River.*

INDEX

Page references in *italic* refer to photographs.